MW00560557

VICTORIA AND ALBERT
MUSEUM
OF
CHILDHOOD

Martha Pullen's Favorite Places Series

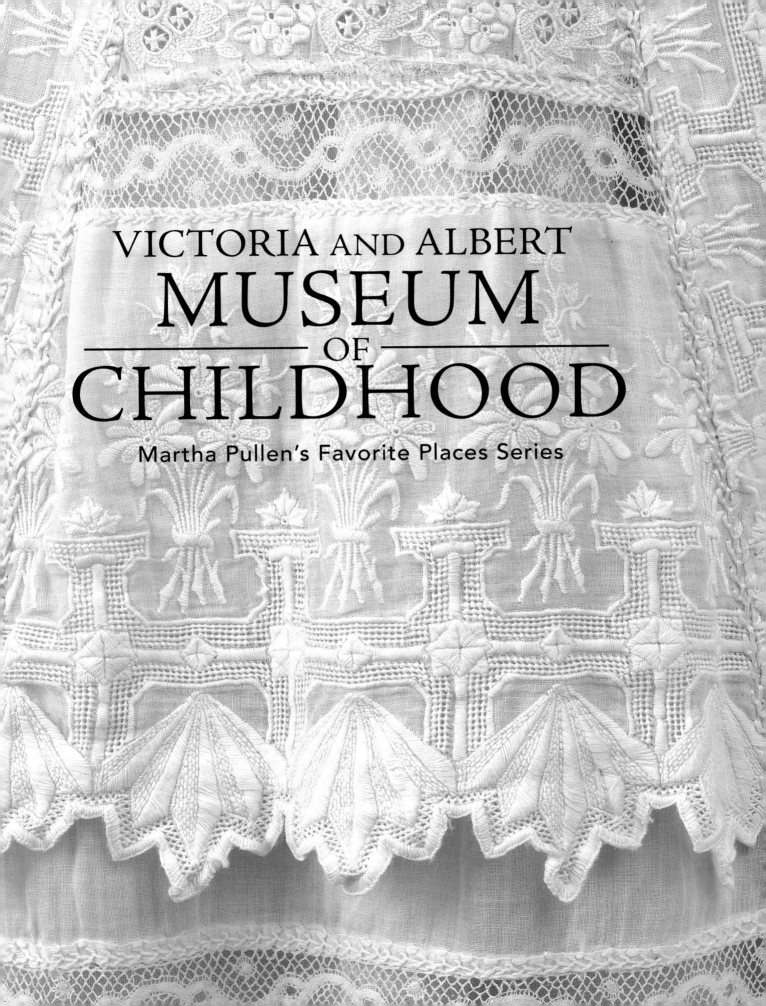

VICTORIA AND ALBERT
MUSEUM
OF
CHILDHOOD

Martha Pullen's Favorite Places Series

The Martha Pullen Company

Publisher: Martha Campbell Pullen, Ph. D.
Editorial Direction by Kathy McMakin
Written by Amelia Johanson with Martha Pullen
Embroidery Art by Angela Pullen Atherton
Copy Editing by Karen Pyne

✦ ✦ ✦ ✦ ✦ ✦ ✦ ✦

The Martha Pullen Company
149 Old Big Cove Road
Brownsboro, Alabama 35741
www.marthapullen.com

V&A Museum of Childhood

All images copyright: V&A Images Museum of Childhood
Editorial Advisor: Noreen Marshall
Photographic Services: Pip Barnard, Ken Jackson,
Clare Johnson and James Stevenson
Image Editing by Clare Johnson
Costume Preparation by Samantha Safer
V&A Publishing: Mark Eastment, Nina Jacobson and
Samantha Safer
The Packing and Transport Team
Diane Lees, Rhian Harris and the staff of the V&A Museum
of Childhood

Hoffman Media, LLC.

President: Phyllis Hoffman
Production Direction by Greg Baugh
Graphic Design by Ronisha B. Quang
Color Correction by Delisa McDaniel
Copy Editing by Nancy Ogburn

✦ ✦ ✦ ✦ ✦ ✦ ✦ ✦

Hoffman Media, LLC.
1900 International Park Drive, Suite 50
Birmingham, Alabama 35243

Copyright © 2008 The Martha Pullen Company, a subsidiary of
Hoffman Media, LLC. All rights reserved. No part of this publication
may be reproduced in any form or by any means, electronic, pho-
tocopy or otherwise without written permission from The Martha
Pullen Company.

Printed in the United States of America

ISBN: 978-0-9794090-7-3

CONTENTS

Dedicated to
Noreen Marshall
Curator of Dress, Doll & Childcare Collections
V&A Museum of Childhood

It is with a great deal of gratitude, admiration and respect that I dedicate this incredible book to my friend for more than 20 years, Noreen Marshall.

photo by Keith Marshall

How could I ever forget my first visit to the Victoria and Albert Museum of Childhood (formerly the Bethnal Green Museum of Childhood)? After having ridden in a black London cab to Bethnal Green, a town in Tower Hamlets, a borough of Greater London, I opened the doors to pure magic. The museum was a fairy tale come to life for me, since all of a sudden I was surrounded by all the Victorian things I love— white children's clothing, doll houses, dolls, antique toys, embroidered clothing, doll carriages and stories galore to go along with them. After touring for what must have been hours, I asked if there were any way I could meet with the children's clothing curator to discuss conducting a photo shoot in the museum for *Sew Beautiful* magazine. The guard called Noreen Marshall's office, and she came upstairs immediately. Our friendship began that very day. Noreen helped organize photo shoots for *Sew Beautiful* and for our first hardcover book on vintage clothing. Later, she guided through the museum two groups of my American sewing friends during a Christmas in London tour. She warmly welcomes my traveling companions and me every time we have an opportunity to visit this fabulous museum. When I asked her if she remembered that first photo shoot for *Sew Beautiful* magazine, she replied, "Of course, I remember that photo shoot, especially the Christmas shots and that rather small boy whose mother admitted it was getting hard to persuade him to continue with modeling clothes – he must be about 25 by now."

Without Noreen's tireless efforts to obtain permission from the V&A Museum board, it is unlikely I would have realized one of the greatest dreams of my professional career – to feature the clothing treasures of my all-time-favorite museum for children in a beautiful book available to my sewing friends the world over. With Noreen's guidance, her eloquent command of the English language and her encyclopaedic knowledge of costume history, we were able to celebrate what lies within the V&A Museum of Childhood. These special pieces are captured in pictures and stories, detailed through the finer points of sewing and brought into the 21st century by the reproduction of some of the actual embroidery designs on CD.

Noreen Marshall was born in 1951 in the seaside town of Lowestoft in Suffolk, England. She read history of art at the University of East Anglia and joined the staff of the V&A Museum in 1974. She has been a curator at the V&A Museum of Childhood since 1978, with a diverse brief in the fine and decorative arts of childhood, including the collections of costume, paintings and furniture. Her recently completed book, *Dictionary of Children's Clothes*, will be published in autumn 2008.

She lives in west London with her husband and two cats, and her interests include the Internet, early music, and book collecting. She is a founding member and Hon Archivist of the Anthony Powell Society, an international literary society, and helped organize its first four international conferences.

I asked Noreen to tell us about herself so you might come to know her more personally. How did she become interested in historic items, and what prompted her to become a museum curator?

I can now see that a lot of little things came together to turn me into a museum curator. From an early age, like most kids, I felt comfortable with hoarding. Not spending money, necessarily, just accumulating glorious amounts of stuff. I had the more usual sorts of collections – stamps, postcards, costume dolls. Although I'm an only child, I come from a big extended family, and some of my cousins passed on toys and books to me. (Hey, that meant my doll Angela was older than I was!) It also gave me an early lesson in recording information (something I do every day of my working life) while figuring out my family tree, plus hearing a lot of memories of the past from my parents and older relatives. While my mother encouraged my passion

for clothes, my father shared my love of the past and its stories, and whenever he could, he took me to look at museums and old buildings.

I also had things I'd picked up, like the hull of a battered wooden toy boat washed up on the seashore. It still sits on a shelf in my office at the museum. When I dug up old clay pipes and pieces of china in the garden, my father told me that once there had been an orchard where our house was. It seems that it was easy to get in there. When he was a child, he and his friends used to come for the apples, and no doubt some adults had used the place to eat their lunch or have a smoke, so I was finding the traces of their presence all those years ago. As my mother said to me when I rang her up to tell her about my first day working at the Museum of Childhood, "You mean they pay you to do something you'd do for pleasure?"

Noreen, this book would not have been possible without your help and expertise. Thank you, sincerely. I am honored to have you as my friend and grateful for your willingness to make this book a reality. I dedicate it to you.

Martha Pullen

RESOURCES

+ www.wikapedia.com
+ www.iht.com/pages/style/index.php
+ http://www.vam.ac.uk/index.html
+ http://www.madeinbirmingham.org
+ Russell, Douglas A., *Costume History and Style*, Prentice-Hall, Inc., ©1983.
+ Black, J. Anderson, Garland, Made & Kennett, Frances, *A History of Fashion*, Orbus Publishing Limited, London ©1975.
+ Toomer, Heather, *Baby Wore White, Robes for Special Occasions 1800-1910*, ©2004 Great Britain: Heather Toomer Antique Lace.
+ Dillmont, Thérése de, *The Complete Encyclopedia of Needlework*, Running Press ©1996.

The Victoria & Albert
MUSEUM OF CHILDHOOD AT BETHNAL GREEN

The Victoria and Albert Museum of Childhood was officially opened by the Prince of Wales as the Bethnal Green Museum on June 24, 1872. At that time, Henry Cole, the director of the South Kensington Museum, hoped that local people would run the museum, but his hopes never materialized. The museum continues to be part of the V&A.

Originally the museum's purpose was regarded as a means of introducing disadvantaged East Enders to the cultural riches of the nation's heritage. Opening displays comprised two collections from the Great Exhibition: Food and animal products and a collection of 18th-century French art on loan from Sir Richard Wallace. The museum continued to display private collections, many of which later served, like the Wallace Collection, as the starting point for other national galleries.

When the museum reopened after the First World War, it not only showcased 19th-century art, but also concentrated on the manufacturing trades common to the local area at the time: silk weaving, shoemaking and furniture making. The transition from this subject matter to the focus on childhood is unofficially attributed to Arthur Sabin, one of the museum's curators. Sabin, who was appointed when the museum reopened, was particularly interested in promoting it as a resource for children. By 1925, he had established both a classroom and a children's section. However, it wasn't until 1974 that the then director of the V&A Sir Roy Strong decided that the museum would officially be dedicated to the subject of childhood. The V&A's collections of children's costume, books, nursery items, art and furni-

ture were relocated and redisplayed in Bethnal Green, alongside the museum's existing toy and doll collection, and the facility was relaunched in 1975 as the Bethnal Green Museum of Childhood. Its collections have continued to evolve, and between 2003 and 2006, the museum secured more than $13 million in funding for a major redevelopment to improve facilities and displays. Temporarily closed for these renovations in 2005 and 2006, the building reopened as the V&A Museum of Childhood in late 2006 to make clear that it exists as part of the V&A family of museums and houses the national childhood collections.

The museum aims to encourage everyone to explore the themes of childhood past and present and to develop an appreciation of creative design through its inspirational collections and programs. The galleries are designed to show the collections in a way that is accessible to adults and children of all ages.

• • • • • • • •

V & A Museum of Childhood at Bethnal Green is located on Cambridge Heath Road, London E2 9PA. It is open to the public 10.00 - 17.45 Monday through Sunday; closed December 24 - 26 and January 1. Admission is free.

CONTRIBUTORS

AMELIA JOHANSON
Co-Author
Associate Editor,
Sew Beautiful Magazine

My earliest memory of sewing anything of substance places me in middle school home economics, working on a blue chambray jacket with a yellow zipper and topstitching. I must have been proud of it to remember it so many years later. Appreciating antiques and vintage clothing came naturally, fostered unknowingly by my grandmother, Mildred Ann Stone. She was a precious part of my childhood, and her antique doll collection is now my collection. Grandma's guest-room closet was full of marvelous clothing, hats and gloves she wore in her younger days. My mother inherited a few pieces she passed on to me along with some of my father's baby clothing. I have gifted many to the Kent State Museum.

Two bachelor's degrees from the University of Missouri in 1986 – in magazine journalism and in home economics with a fashion emphasis – prepared me for my first job as assistant to the fashion editor at the Cleveland *Plain Dealer* and then as the fashion writer at *The Columbus Dispatch*. When my husband and I moved to Huntsville, Alabama so that he could pursue an aerospace career, I learned of a niche publication called *Sew Beautiful* magazine. I was transfixed by the lacework, heirloom clothing and finely-dressed Southern children. It spoke to that little girl in awe of her grandmother's keepsakes, the pre-teen in sewing class, and the journalist who had aspired to a magazine career. I was blessed to become a part of it and over the past 20 years have served as editor, writer and designer for *Sew Beautiful* and many Martha Pullen books.

MARTHA PULLEN
Co-Author
President,
Martha Pullen Company

Martha Campbell Pullen, Ph.D. is founder and president of Martha Pullen Company, which started as a fabric shop in Huntsville, Alabama. In 1981, two months after opening her shop, Martha realized that the best way to secure quality laces and fabrics for customers was to import them from Europe herself. She produced a mail-order catalog and in 1987 started publishing *Sew Beautiful* magazine. The Martha Pullen School of Art Fashion was started because of her love of teaching as was the television series, *Martha's Sewing Room* for PBS. She has had the pleasure of teaching sewing on six continents. She and her incredible colleagues have collaborated on producing over 50 books in the sewing arena.

In 2004 Martha Pullen Company became a subsidiary of Birmingham-based Hoffman Media, a merger that freed up Martha to focus on a career-long dream – to share centuries-old garments with the world. Her Favorite Places Series brings celebrated museum clothing collections to the heirloom sewing-enthusiasts. The accompanying CD's of actual period embroideries reproduced from the featured garments let her meet one of her longtime objectives – to mesh heirloom inspiration with modern sewing technology.

Martha was born in Morristown, New Jersey; however she grew up in Scottsboro, Alabama. Her degrees are from The University of Alabama.

Martha is in the American Sewing Guild Hall of Fame. She was named a national Daughter of Distinction of the Daughters of the American Revolution, an

CONTRIBUTORS

honor she shares with Elizabeth Dole and Janet Reno. She was named Huntsville/Madison County Chamber of Commerce Executive of the Year. She has been a nominee for *Inc.* magazine's executive of the year. She is a member of Rotary International and the Optimist Club. Martha was presented the Golden Needle Award from the Schmetz Needle Company of Germany and Euro-notions. She is the wife of retired implant dentist Joe Ross Pullen, the mother of five and the grandmother of 17. Martha has volunteered with the Southern Baptist International Mission Board in Africa, Jamaica, and Brazil. She is a devoted Christian and gives the credit for her business to God.

PIP BARNARD
Photographer

Pip Barnard has worked as one of the V&A's Photographers for many years. He has created images for a number of very different V&A publications, from *Gothic: Art for England 1400-1547* to *Dictionary of Children's Clothes.*

CLARE JOHNSON

Clare Johnson was born in London, UK. She studied graphic design at Camberwell School of Art. Clare worked for many years in advertising before doing digital imaging, pre press, design and retouching for the V&A.

SAMANTHA SAFER

Samantha Safer was born in New Jersey, USA. She studied art history and fashion history at Bard College in Annandale-on-Hudson, New York, before moving to London in 2004 to work as the assistant curator at the Fashion and Textile Museum. Before this, she gained experience at P.S.1 MoMa and the Brooklyn Museum of Art. Samantha gained her master's degree in the History of Design from the Royal College of Art and Victoria and Albert Museum, London in 2007. Recently she has contributed to a book on Lucile, Lady Duff Gordon being published by the V&A in spring 2009. She also teaches fashion history and theory at university level as well as freelances for the Learning and Interpretation department and Publishing of the V&A.

PREFACE

As a little girl, I dreamed of one day traveling to England. I was an avid reader and devoured books about Buckingham Palace, Big Ben, Windsor Palace and Westminster Abby. I listened with great interest to Campbell family history and about my ancestors coming to this country from Scotland in the 1600s. Both sides of my mother's family, the Bakers and the Greens, were from England. When Shakespeare's plays were presented to me for the first time, in high school, my love of "all things English" intensified. Later, in college, I majored in theatre and even had an opportunity to portray Paulina in The Winter's Tale. My English minor would then take me to North Carolina and Georgia to teach, what else, British literature.

Chill bumps went up and down my spine the first time my plane landed at Heathrow Airport, and I realized that my lifelong dream of visiting England had finally come true. I was so excited, I could hardly breathe. I still vividly remember the "way in" and "way out" signs in the airport; how peculiar they seemed to someone who is used to seeing "enter" and "exit." But most of all, I remember an overwhelming sense of coming "home" when I finally set foot on English soil.

During this first trip to England, I must have purchased 30 baby dresses at the New Caledonian Market in Bermondsey and from antiques dealers along Portobello Road; Stephen Lunn's shop is still one of my favorites. Upon realizing my absolute enchantment with antique baby clothes, one of the vendors said to me, "Have you visited the Bethnal Green Museum of Childhood? I think you must go since you love baby clothes so much." I couldn't hail a black cab fast enough.

I spent all afternoon touring the museum, and felt as if I were on overload. I desperately tried to memorize each detail of every garment, every doll dress and doll house. Once I saw the "The Bin Dress" hanging proudly inside a glass case, I was totally smitten. The history behind that glorious dress (it was recovered from a trash bin) made me realize that I was far from alone in recognizing the beauty and importance of these finely made antique garments. After several hours in the museum, I begrudgingly pulled myself away, but not without first arranging to meet Noreen Marshall, the curator of dress, doll and childcare collections; our relationship through the years is, in part, what led to this book.

My love of heirloom sewing, and everything I've done in my business to develop heirloom sewing by machine techniques, has been rooted in the fine craftsmanship of antique clothing, primarily what I call the "white clothes." I established Martha Pullen Company after studying these historical pieces to help bring the delicate art of yesterday's sewing and design ideas into our world of technologically advanced machines. Today we can quickly and easily replicate the look of the hand embroidery that not that long ago was so labor intensive. I hope that through this book and the machine embroidery CDs, which are available separately, you will be

inspired to create the heirloom-sewn dress of your dreams.

Bringing this book to you has been my dream since I first set foot in the Victoria and Albert Museum of Childhood, and in putting it together, I encountered a bit of irony I feel compelled to share before you delve into its contents. My mother went to college at Florence State Teacher's College in the mid-1930s. Going away to college was almost unheard of in that part of Alabama, but my grandparents, a school teacher and a farmer/carpenter, had saved every penny so that Mama could further her education. The first time she had an opportunity to visit downtown Florence, she was enthralled with the city's bakery. She looked through the glass window at a display of beautiful pineapple rolls and promised herself right then and there that she would save enough of her semester's spending money to purchase some of those rolls at Christmastime to take home to the family. My promise that first day I looked into the glass cases at the museum in England was to somehow bring the beauty "home" to you. And the irony? When I returned to the museum last winter to start on this book, the very first garment Noreen showed me was a blue silk coat embroidered with, what else, pineapples.

I am deeply indebted to Noreen Marshall, Mark Eastment and Nina Jacobson for giving us permission to bring this book to you. I am very appreciative to the whole staff both in London and here in the United States for their untiring efforts to get this book into your hands. It is my great pleasure to share with you my passion for the V&A Museum of Childhood, a journey that began many years ago with my first visit to this magical place.

Martha Pullen

The Bin Dress

English, 1900-1920

"A scrap of paper laid in the box with the lace or tacked to the back of the secretary preserves at least the outline. The christening dress, the baby blanket that the grandmother knit—all need help of paper and ink if they are to carry an intelligible message to the next generation."
— "Labels," *Congregationalist and Christian World*, March 14, 1903

The "Bin Dress" was so named by the museum because apparently it was found in a dustbin (or dumpster, in American English) in the Old Welwyn/Codicote area of England. A member of the family of donors salvaged the gown from impending doom and subsequently used it for a number of christenings in the family, beginning with Mr. and Mrs. Fredrick Hazel's children, Mary, born 1934, Frederick, born 1935, and Christine, born 1951. In the next generation it was worn by Mary's children, Alan, born 1955, Martin, born 1957, Susan, born 1960 and Jon, born 1961; then Frederick's children, Karen, born 1958, Jeoff, born 1960, Jackie, born 1962 and Diane, born 1963. Finally, the gown was worn by Christine's daughter, Emily, born 1979, although not by her son, Daniel, presumably because of the feeling some modern families have against dressing a boy in a gown.

The gown is fine white linen with a round drawstring neck and full, wrist-length sleeves. The bodice is a bold design of mitered insertion – one large lace zigzag overlapping a lace V to create a center diamond. Two strips of slightly narrower lace insertion are placed vertically 1-inch apart at the sides of the bodice beneath the lace zigzag. Four French knots are embroidered in the center of the diamond. The remaining sections of white fabric are either filled with rows of 1/8-inch-wide tucks or embellished with zigzags of featherstitching. The long sleeves that extend from a slightly dropped shoulder are finished at the wrist with embroidered ribbon slot and a slightly gathered 3/8-inch-wide lace edging, which also finishes the neckline. Entredeux is set into the shoulder seams.

The skirt is a series of panels, each tucked at the top to gather the fullness into the ribbon-slot waistband. The two front panels are flanked with ribbon slot and joined to a single strip of lace insertion down the center front. Each of these panels is embellished with three mitered Vs of lace insertion between Vs of tucked fabric. The two side panels are embellished toward the bottom with two sections of five pintucks shaped into a slight downward curve. A self-fabric frill

is embellished with a row of French lace insertion and a row of flat lace edging, and is gathered into the ribbon slot at the bottom of the skirt with release tucks. The ribbon slot throughout the gown is run with pink ribbons, which were modern replacements, as were the two pink ribbon bows tacked to the sides of the waist.

The gown fastens in back with three buttons and stitched buttonholes, along with the free ends of the ribbon which are tied at the waist. It is 36-inches long.

Misc.217 and A-1982
Gift of Christine Boardman on behalf of her parents,
Mr. and Mrs. Frederick Hazel

Creative Inspiration
Use ribbon slot or beading throughout a christening gown design so that it can be made gender neutral simply by changing the ribbons from pink to blue.

Pomegranates and Pineapples Coat

British, 1880-1895

"Silk costumes naturally take precedence of all others now that nearly every kind of plain silken fabric is so fashionable."

— "Autumn Novelties At Les Grands Magasins Du Louvre, Paris,"
Myra's Journal of Dress and Fashion, (October 1, 1886)

The front of this silk child's coat is distinguishable only by the positioning of the collar. The placement of the box pleats and the seaming of the two-piece sleeve are virtually identical, front and back; closer examination reveals that the center-front panel is a faux pleat concealing a placket, which opens the full length of the coat and fastens with hooks and eyes.

Documentation describes the piece as "petrol blue silk twill, lined throughout with dark cream, figured cotton in a textured serpentine pattern and embroidered in the style of the arts and crafts movement." This movement is associated with William Morris's work, which was concerned that objects be useful, beautiful and enhance the lives of both the craftsman and the owner – an admirable ideal, but quite difficult to achieve. In England, the movement mutated so that only the wealthy could afford the craftsmanship and decorative work. It runs tandem with the aesthetic movement, during which everything was consciously sought out for

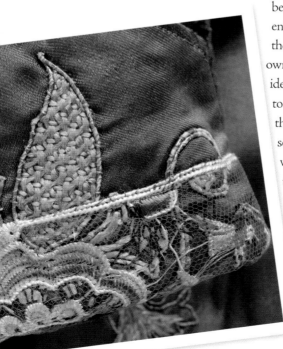

its beauty, not its practicality. The beauty of this garment is undeniable; its function as a coat although obvious is perhaps diminished somewhat since the fragility of silk is not suited to the elements.

The box pleats, collar and sleeve edges are richly worked in silk threads with flowers, fruit and leaves in hand-stitched embroidery and laid work in cream, coral, purple and shades of blue, pink, and green. The stitches include satin stitch, featherstitch, herringbone stitch, detached buttonhole stitch, blanket stitch, and tied cross-stitch; some of the motifs are also decorated with beadwork. Couched gold thread outlines much of the embroidery, so that the coat is somewhat ecclesiastical looking. The embroidery ends 5-inches above the bottom edge of the coat.

The front pleats and collar are edged with split blanket stitch in coral silk thread, and the hems of the sleeves and the top of the neck front have been covered with strips of ornamental machine-embroidered insertion encased in netting. It can be assumed that this was added later to hide the edges that were fraying slightly at the time.

The garment is constructed in six panels and is box-pleated from neck to hem at front (three pleats), at the sides (two pleats) and back (three pleats). The pleats are 2-inches wide and secured with rather crude stitches, which are hidden beneath the folds. The center panel, or faux box pleat, is a separate fabric section, which was cut from the selvedge. The selvedge is turned back 1/4-inch at the pleat fold and secured with hand stitches. The opposite side is turned back 7/8-inch to the interior of the coat on the front opening and hand-stitched to the lining.

At the neck and waist edges, the panel is turned under and secured with hand topstitching.

The illusion in the garment is that the bodice is a separate piece. Actually, toppers of silk, their edges turned under and secured with hand-picked stitches, are applied between each box pleat, adding an additional layer for warmth and implying a dropped-waist construction.

On the contrary, the lining, front and back, is cut in two pieces to create a waist seam, but the side panels run from underarm to hem as one piece on both the interior and outer layers of the coat. Rather than construct a second lining and place one inside the other, the seamstress layered the lining with the coat pieces before construction. The interior seam allowances are finished with a hand whipstitch. The hem is finished with a 2-inch facing of the lining material. The length of the front opening from neck to hem is 20-1/2-inches.

B.17-1998
Gift of Mrs. Jocelyn A. Howden

Creative Inspiration
Edge box pleats with contrast stitching to stabilize the folds with decorative flair. Use a hand or machine embroidery stitch.

Corded Carrying Coat Ensemble

French, 1850-1900

"One thing that has struck me much in Paris, and most agreeably, and that is the appearance of the children. The children of the rich are beautifully dressed, and are accompanied by excellent attendants. The number of beautiful babies you meet in the streets, so exquisitely dressed, has the same effect upon one that the lovely flowers do, that you meet at the corner of every street."
— Letter VIII, *The Child's Friend and Family Magazine*, May 1, 1850

Museum records reveal that the Scottish baby Andrew Crookson, born in 1895, was probably the recipient of this elaborate ensemble. It consists of a plain carrying coat, a highly decorated cape and similarly adorned bonnet and booties; Victorians would have called them "boots," and only one of the pair has survived.

There is no specific mention that these pieces were intended for a christening, however the ornate nature of the cape and accessories implies that were the case. Once dressed in his finery, little Andrew would have been carried to the church by his mother or a nursemaid. And although today a baby would wear a christening ensemble only once before it is packed away, many Victorians held a more practical view of apparel. Most likely, Andrew would have been bundled for outings in this set until it no longer fit.

The plain coat has a round neck and fastens at the yoke front with three hooks and stitched loops. The full-length sleeves are gathered into a turned-back cuff. The flared skirt is pleated into the yoke and finished above the hem with three horizontal tucks. The garment is lined with hand-quilted silk, except for the sleeves, which are lined with plain silk. The center back length of the coat is 35-1/2 inches.

The layers of flouncing around the edges of the cape and turned-down collar imitate similar elaboration popular in women's gowns of the period. A deep triple frill of lace is layered atop pleated and ribbon-edged silk muslin, and pinked silk. The body of the cape is trimmed completely around with a ruched cream ribbon in a looped pattern, and the cape is lined with silk throughout. The garment fastens at the neck front with a metal hook and loop beneath streamers and loops of broad silk satin ribbon that augment the frothy effect. The center back length of the cape is 24-1/2-inches.

The bootie is lace over corded silk lined with white linen. The sole is white kid leather and the insole is of brushed cotton. The top is scalloped with ruched ribbon and trimmed with a rosette of looped ivory satin baby ribbon on the vamp. The bootie laces with a length of ivory satin ribbon.

The crown of the matching bonnet is covered with ruched corded silk on a buckram foundation and is lined with cream silk. The brim is made of lace edging between three layers of silk muslin. The neck edging is lace over one layer of silk muslin, and the neckband is trimmed in back with an ivory satin bow. There is a wide cockade of silk muslin near the top of the brim. When worn, the bonnet would have been secured with a drawstring of cream ribbon and tying strings of ivory satin.

Misc.779:1-4-1986
Gift of Mrs. M. Mead

Pressed Roses Coat

English, 1879

"White is indeed quite the favourite colour for all dressy out-door costumes, and some of these are extremely elegant."
— "Modes for Children," *Myra's Journal*, July 1, 1888

"Children seem to be devoted for some time to come to two kinds of toilettes – the princesse dress for girls from five to eleven years old, and the English frock for little boys from the time they begin to walk to four and a half years of age."
— "Paris Fashions," *Harper's Bazaar*, August 25, 1877

The princess line became a standard silhouette for the girl's toilette in the 1870s, and this lovely example of the fitted construction was made in 1879. It was worn by Lady Beatrice Egerton and her sisters, the young daughters of the Third Earl of Ellesmere, according to museum records. The coat buttons from neck to hem and has an inverted pleat at the center back of the skirt, which implies a bustle. It owes its beauty in part to machine work; the cotton fabric is a machine-quilted rose print, and the lace is a machine-made broderie anglaise.

It is exquisitely constructed with beautifully executed hand sewing, and despite being worn by several children in the family more than a century ago, it remains in nearly pristine condition.

The front of the coat is cut in two pieces, 25-inches long from neckline front to where the Swiss insertion is attached at the hem. The neckline is finished with a 3/4-inch-wide bias band, secured with hand whipstitches on the inside and topped with minute machine stitches. A gathered French bobbin lace, 5/8-inch wide, is hand-whipped to the top of the bias band. A ruched portrait collar is applied on top of the basic neckline treatment. The collar is ruched for a depth of 1-1/2-inches in five rows of hand-gathering stitches and applied to the coat with tacking stitches taken along each row of the ruching stitches.

The lace pattern reflects the popularity of the Greek key motif – two hemstitched lines form a structured path around small rectangles of alternating eyelet and embroidered flowers.

The two-piece long sleeves, cut with a top panel and an underarm panel so that a seam runs down the front and back, are finished like the bottom of the coat.

The back of the coat is beautifully tailored into a princess line made from three panels – two at the sides and a center panel made up of two pieces of fabric seamed together. The center panel is seamed straight down the middle from neckline to 13-inches into the coat where the seam opens to reveal a 5-inch-wide inverted pleat. The curved princess seams positioned to either side of center back also open 13-inches into the coat by means of 3-inch tucks that are folded toward the coat center. This line of construction fashions a bustle effect prevalent at the time. In the 1870s, girls' dresses followed the adult line with their back-drawn draperies and the bustle; the effect was often tight cramping devoid of youthfulness, though this is not the case with this pretty piece.

T.162-1962
Gift of The Dowager Lady Rochdale

Chain-Stitch Carrying Cape
English, 1870-1880

"Emma had the country girl's usual wide experience of baby welfare, and was proud to give me the information I required. 'How often should we change her nightdress, Emma?' I asked. The reply was immediate and unequivocal – 'Oh, a baby always looks to have a clean one twice a week'. She knew also the odd names for the odd garments that babies wore in that era – such as 'bellyband' (about a yard of flannel that was swathed round and round and safety-pinned on) and 'barracoat' . . ."

— *A London Home in the 1890s*, M V Hughes (Oxford University Press, 1978)

Well-to-do Victorian babies wouldn't have ventured outdoors unless wrapped in an elaborate cloak or mantle. Poorer families would have relied on a shawl or a blanket to protect their babies from exposure. The coddling was not unfounded. Foremost child-rearing expert, Ada S. Ballin, who penned *From Cradle to School, A Book for Mothers*, advised: "Exposure to cold is especially fatal to young infants, who not only, in proportion to the smallness of their bodies, lose heat more readily than adults, but are also less able to supply the loss of heat by the recuperative nature of their own bodies." She followed with the claim that "countless murders have been caused by the practice of leaving bare the neck and arms of the poor little shivering atoms of humanity."

This baby carrying cape is cream twilled cashmere. The garment has a turned-down collar and pelisse over the cloak. All three layers are lavishly worked in a regal, chain-stitched embroidery design of cream silk threads enhanced with cream silk appliquéd leaves and flowers. The pelisse cape has a double tassel of cream silk at each corner.

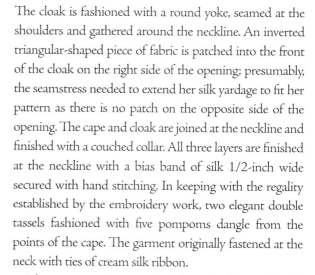

The cloak is fashioned with a round yoke, seamed at the shoulders and gathered around the neckline. An inverted triangular-shaped piece of fabric is patched into the front of the cloak on the right side of the opening; presumably, the seamstress needed to extend her silk yardage to fit her pattern as there is no patch on the opposite side of the opening. The cape and cloak are joined at the neckline and finished with a couched collar. All three layers are finished at the neckline with a bias band of silk 1/2-inch wide secured with hand stitching. In keeping with the regality established by the embroidery work, two elegant double tassels fashioned with five pompoms dangle from the points of the cape. The garment originally fastened at the neck with ties of cream silk ribbon.

Like many carrying capes, both layers (pelisse and cloak) are faced along the front edges with elongated silk triangles so that if the garment flies open, the whole appears to be silk lined. The cheat is that the bulk of the lining is a cream twill, which would have been a more affordable and durable fabric.

Misc.609-1988
Gift of The Royal College of Art

Creative Inspiration
Achieve a look similar to chain stitch by using machine embroidery or by couching cord. Work the decorative framework over a satin foundation for an elegant textural appliqué.

White Christmas Coat and Capelet

English, 1865

"The Christmas festivities, in which children take so large a share and in which they so much delight, cannot be properly celebrated without new dresses for the occasions; at least this is the generally received opinion amongst the children, and the materials now in vogue for children's best dresses are so pretty and so varied and the styles in which they are made up so becoming to childish figures, that mamas may well be forgiven if they abandon their own or prudent views, and allow themselves to be easily converted to those of their little daughters on this important point."
— "Modes for Children," *Myra's Journal of Dress and Fashion*, December 1, 1886

What Americans think of as the Christmas plant was brought to the United States in the 1820s by Joel Roberts Poinsett, America's Mexican ambassador and an amateur botanist. Exactly when the Poinsettia made its way to England doesn't appear to be as well documented. Evidence does suggest that the plant flourished at some point during Queen Victoria's reign. After her death in 1901, the *Christian Advocate* paid tribute to the monarch in an article titled "Flowers that Grew by Royal Command." In it, an unknown author writes, "The palmhouse is brightened by the scarlet flowers of the poinsettia, which are cut in quantities for vase and table decorations."

This child's coat, dated 1865 (midway through Victoria's reign), establishes that the plant was known in the country by the middle of the century. The largest motif of the all-over embroidery is a realistic rendition of poinsettia foliage worked at the corners of the coat and the removable capelet. The design above the poinsettia looks to be a variation of a columbine next to sprays of phlox. The sharp, scalloped borders are a series of petals and eyelets worked around Indian-like shapes of hemstitching filled in with satin-stitch vines, rays and dots and all-over single eyelets. The border design continues around the coat and capelet and is topped with a continuous vine of phlox. The capelet and coat are worked in the same embroidery design. The collar is a similar yet slightly smaller version of the border embroidery. The edges of the left side of the coat, and those on the collar and capelet are scalloped in buttonhole stitch. The sleeve edges are finished in a row of satin stitching next to a row of hemstitching.

The embroidery is technically sound, and close examination with the aid of a magnifying glass reveals that it may be a mixture of hand and machine work. Curator Noreen Marshall suspects that it is Indian in origin, a less expensive facsimile rather than authentic Ayrshire embroidery. At the time this coat was constructed, British families could buy Indian embroidery at shops which specialized in yardage of this kind.

The cuffs are a bit of a cheat, which is disappointing on a garment that is otherwise so perfectly rendered. Each is a single layer of embroidery worked in a trapezoid shape and simply attached to the front of the sleeve for a mock cuff. These half-cuffs are joined to the hemstitched edge of the sleeve and tacked back. The coat fabric is ribbed piqué run horizontally.

The interior side seams of the skirt of the coat are French and are slightly hidden within an inverted pleat at the side seam. Six buttonholes line up on both sides of the coat, although no buttons remain with the coat. Sometimes the fastenings were so regarded they were often removed and applied to another garment. These were likely a kind of two-sided shank button, which would have fastened through both sets of buttonholes.

The capelet is finished in a star shape so that the back ends in a point; it is tailored with two shoulder darts, each 3-inches long and placed 3-inches from the front opening.

T.221-1969
T.21A-1969
Gift of Mrs. Lucy L. Hardman

Lavender Blue Child's Cape

English, 1870-1880

"I am a very little girl, but am growing larger every year, and by and by, I hope to be more useful than I am now. Father works hard, out in the fields, and mother works so hard at home; for she has a deal to do among so many of us What a many pennies it must take to buy all our clothes, and bonnets, and shoes."

"Mother says time is as good as money; and that, if I cannot help her much, I should not hinder her by being untidy; so I keep everything about me as tidy as I can. I put my chair in the corner when I have done with it, that nobody may tumble over it. I try to learn to sew a little."
— Careful Susan," *London Child's Companion,* reprinted in *The Youth's Companion* March 30, 1838

Although capes fall in and out of favor at the whims of fashion, they once held a prominent place in the feminine toilette. Victorians regarded the cape as essential outerwear, as likely to be wrapped over a baby's christening gown as over her mother's finery. Unlike a structured coat, the cape could be draped gently over a gown with full sleeves and ornate décolletage with less chance of crushing the effects.

This girl's cape of pale puce silk is figured with a self-colored pattern of vertical waving stems and pinnate leaves. It is lined and piped in turquoise silk satin and layered with batting for added warmth. The rounded, turned-down collar is cut from the turquoise silk satin and the double shoulder cape, from the puce silk. Vertical slits with decorative external flaps are fashioned for armholes. The flaps are lined with the turquoise silk satin. Tying strings of broad pale turquoise ribbon (one missing) secure the cape at the neck. The cape measures 32-1/2-inches long from the back neckline to the hem. Gores to shape the cape are tucked into the neckline at the shoulder point and radiate out to 7-inches wide at the hem. Back fullness is gathered into the back neckline with a 2-inch center pleat flanked by two 1-inch pleats. The lining is secured with hand running stitches all the way along the interior of the piping. The cape was entirely hand stitched. It was purchased for the museum in a sale of costume and textiles at Christie's Auction House in London.

B.448-1994

Posies Carrying Cape

United Kingdom, 1860-1869

"Bassinettes. High-Class baby Carriages. T. Elderkin's are all made of best materials and by most skilled labour. T. Elderkin has long been considered one of the best makers and had a reputation to lose. From 35s to 10 pounds 10s. Elderkin, Maker, Oxford St. Manchester"
— Advertisement, *Myra's Journal of Dress*, August 1, 1887

The term carrying cape propagated from the idea that a nursemaid physically carried the baby during family outings, a practice that when combined with the nursemaid's long skirts – the accepted mode of women's dress – concerned the medical community. Because many nursemaids were not much more than children themselves, it was not unheard of for them to trip over their hems and risk dropping their little charges. Still, wealthy families would have wrapped their babies in a cape of this sort even if the child were being taken for a family carriage ride, and the name persisted. An embellished carrying cape was undoubtedly a garment of status, as well as a provision for baby's warmth.

On this piece, the capelet is fixed with five rows of ruching placed 1/2-inch apart. The outer layer of the capelet is one piece; the inner layer is a separate round yoke and lining of twill. As is typical of most carrying capes in the Victoria and Albert collection, this one is faced just inside the front openings of the capelet and the cloak with large triangles of silk; the remainder of the lining is twill for both practicality and durability.

Three pairs of grosgrain ribbons close the cape, attached at the neckline, at the yoke of the cloak and 1-inch below from the yoke. A belt loop of sorts is stitched to the turned-back facing of the capelet at the point that corresponds to the bottom tie on the cloak. The tie would have been threaded through the loop to keep the capelet from flying up or being pulled out of position. For conservation, presumably, there is only one of these belt loops, as it does not appear that one was ever stitched to the opposite side.

The capelet and the cape are joined at the neckline with a bias band, 3/8-inch wide and hand stitched to secure on the inside edge. The band is topped with a line of hand featherstitching. The cloak is a circular yoke to which the remainder of the garment was hand gathered. A single line of gathering stitches to create one row of ruching remains in the cloak, and the seam is bridged with a rather heavy piping. The ecru-on-ecru silk floss embroidery follows the lines of the capelet and the cloak. The design is a running scallop of posies on a vine with floral sprigs tossed about on the interior. The capelet is 23-inches long; the cloak is 38-inches long. Only recently has the cape come to be a short garment.

Misc.501-1984
Gift of Hilda Dorothy Smythe

Bris Gown Cape and Barracoat

British, 1870-79; Cape and Barracoat, British, 1929

"A Boon to Infant and Mother.
Roberts' HYGROSCOPIC or Patent Swans Down Diaper and Towel.
This material is a perfect absorbent, possessing comforting, cleanly, and antiseptic properties.
Has received the unqualified approval of Medical Man and Professional Nurses.
It is more durable than Linen Diaper at half the cost.
T. Roberts& Co., 22 Tib St., Manchester
Write for Sample Diaper (Free by Post Seven Stamps) mentioning Myra's Journal."
— Advertisement, *Myra's Journal of Dress and Fashion*, September 1, 1887

Jewish families mark the beginning of a male child's religious life with a Bris Milah, or circumcision ceremony. The pieces of this ensemble were specially constructed to be worn by a Jewish child for this milestone. Records indicate the gown, the earliest piece, was most likely made by the donor's maternal grandmother, Minna Paiba, for her eldest son, born some time during the 1870s. Subsequently, it was worn by her other sons; her grandson, the donor, Kenneth David Rubens, born in 1929 (at which point the cape and barracoat were added); and by his eldest son born in 1962. According to Mr. Rubens, the Jewish Museum in London

was not interested in these garments because there is nothing notably Jewish about them except their provenance. Without the documentation, they would be taken for christening clothes, as would another bris gown of about 1900, which the museum has recently acquired.

The hand-embroidered cape is an ivory ribbed rayon textile. The corners of the collar, pelisse and cape are worked with a floral spray-and-bow design in ivory silk floss. The edges of the pelisse are finished in a compound scallop that somewhat resembles petals or a partial flower with an embroidered dot or pistal at each center. The scallop is repeated on the collar. The cape is constructed around a round yoke and closes with two buttons and button loops near the neckline and a wider ribbon of ivory silk positioned midway down the cape. The cape back length is 27-inches.

The gown is fine white linen, the silhouette a central princess-line panel made up of horizontal insertions, both Swiss and French styles, and machine-embroidered Swiss edging. All the laces are secured to the garment with featherstitching. The three deep frills on the panel are machine-embroidered edging worked in a stacked design – sprays of daisy bouquets above cross motifs, which are framed by a simulation of drawn threadwork that pours into an edge of fan-shaped medallions. The crosses could be mistaken for Christian symbolism and might explain the Jewish Museum's reluctance to acquire the ensemble. The frills are applied slightly gathered over flat linen panels

that alternate with sections of the Swiss and French insertions. The Swiss insertion is a design of embroidered flowers and stylized leaves that incorporate three eyelets filled with cross medallions. The significance of three in Christian dress symbolizes the Father, Son and Holy Spirit, another curiosity in a garment that was designed for a Jewish ceremony.

The alternating pattern of French and Swiss lace fills in the bodice area for nine rows. The robings are from the deep embroidered edging mitered into the bottom frill and applied so that they gradually narrow as they approach the shoulders; this compromises some of the embroidery work. The back of the garment consists of a plain bodice and a gathered skirt finished at the bottom with a series of three tucks, a strip of Swiss edging and three more tucks above a deep hem. The wrist-length sleeves are inserted with a tiny double entredeux and finished with cuffs of Swiss insertion with a French lace edging ruffle. The same edging trims the neckline. Drawstrings fasten the gown in back at the neckline and the waist.

The flannel petticoat, or barracoat, is from the same collection and is worn beneath the more elaborate gown. The wraparound design is made of cream flannelette. The sleeveless bodice ties at the side with a silk ribbon and is finished around the edges with a bias binding of silk. The attached skirt opens down the side and ties in two places with silk ribbon. The edges of the skirt are embroidered in a pretty scallop design alternating two different styles and widths of compound scallops; next to each repeat of the wider scallop is a stemmed flower. The wrap design of the barracoat is perfectly suited to its purpose, as it could be easily opened and closed during the ceremony. The back length is 28-inches.

Misc.561, 562, 563-1985
Gift of Kenneth Rubens

Creative Inspiration

Combine vintage details – tone-on-tone embroidery and silk bows and bindings – with the softness of baby flannel in a wraparound gown that is comfortable, practical and heirloom in nature.

Ribbons and Roses Double Cape
English, 1887

"Outdoor costumes for small folks this winter will all be most cosy little garments. Long cloaks in plain and fancy clothes, warmly lined, and trimmed with velvet, fur, and astrakhan, and long paletots will be generally worn."
— "Clothing for Infants," *Myra's Journal*, November 1, 1888

Two baby girls were blessed to have worn this elaborate cape – Hilda Dorothy, born 1887, and Edith Florence, born 1891. The cape was made by a family friend who must have spent hours making it. The large floral motif is embroidered nearly from top to bottom, repeats on either side of the cloak and capelet, and trails around to the back of both pieces in a vine propagated with buds. It is unusual to find embellishment on the back of a carrying cape that required a significant investment of time and effort. That area of the garment was rarely seen because a baby wearing it would almost always have been cradled in someone's arms. A smaller variation of the vine is also embroidered around the collar.

The embroidery motif resembles the elegant needlework of the French Rococo period, and although it is relatively large for a child's garment, it seems appropriate to this piece.

In keeping with the ambitious embroidery design, an elaborate 4-inch-wide English netting lace is gathered around the collar and capelet. Wide silk ribbon ties, 1-1/2-inches wide, are placed equal distances apart to close the garment in three places – at the neck and at two places on the cloak. The cloak is applied to a round yoke. It is not gathered where it joins to the yoke, and there is a triangular-shaped inset on the left front side, presumably to extend the fabric to fit the pattern. When worn, this patch is concealed underneath the capelet. Both pieces are lined in twill. The capelet is 30-inches long; the cloak is 36-inches long with a circumference of 67-inches.

Misc.219-1979
Gift of Miss H. D. Smythe

Pink Printed Spring Pelisse Robe and Tippet

United Kingdom, 1840

"Mother do tell me what father means when he says he will show us the green spots of this golden world during the summer?" said a little girl who was sitting at her mother's knee performing her morning task of needlework.

"It is," replied her mother, "a favorite expression of his, and arose from my once relating to him some May-day festivities, which took place in the village of Bloomingdale where I passed some of my early years."

"Oh! Thank you, mother. I love to hear you talk of the days you spent in Devonshire: I should think it must be a lovely place, for you always appear so happy when speaking of it."

— "Green Spots in This Golden World," *The Child's Friend and Family Magazine,*
November 1, 1843

Museum documentation describes this exquisite garment as "a Pelisse robe for a girl. Pink/white striped printed cotton with brown triangle motifs, England, about 1840." To the sewing eye, it is so much more, refined with an assortment of details that separate it from an ordinary garment. The level of hand construction rivals machine work, with each stitch precisely placed and each piece cut, gathered and fit to perfect form. For example, where the stripes lie at an angle, they are at exactly the same angle whether on the cuff, the collar or the tibbet. Meticulous hand featherstitching marks the garment throughout and is equally impressive; it is used both decoratively – topping seams, edging the belt and tippet and trimming the bows – and functionally – securing the knife pleats at the shoulders and the facings around the edges.

The seam that joins the collar to the garment is finished with a bias binding, which serves as a casing for a draw cord. The removable tippet is worn beneath the collar; the edges of both are finished with a narrow cotton facing, which is turned under and caught with featherstitching worked from the right side. Flat ecru Swiss edging is applied around the finished edges with tiny faggoting.

Each side of the pelisse robe front is one piece from shoulder to the hem. The fullness at the top is ruched at the shoulder from the armscye to the neckline and is secured with two 3/8-inch bands of bias fabric piped on either side and topped with featherstitching. One band is positioned toward the front shoulder and curves into the

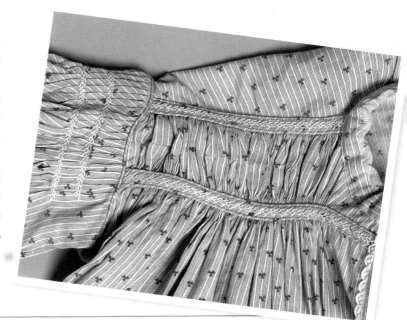

front opening of the coat; the other lies to the back of the shoulder and is set straight into the neckline. The back of the robe joins the front at this band. A casing and draw cord runs across the interior of the back at waist level to ease in the fullness. A 1-1/4-inch-wide waist belt covers this effect. The belt joins with a hook-and-eye closure in front, which would be hidden beneath the tippet when worn. Two pockets are cut into the fabric of the front and finished with edging to match that on the rest of the garment.

The full sleeves, which are set in with piping, are descended from a gigot silhouette and are shaped at the top with nearly two dozen knife pleats secured in two rows of featherstitching. The deep cuff suggests a turned-back design, although it is a separate piece cut on the bias. The cuff is finished in kind, and like the pelisse, beautifully mitered at the points. The garment opens all the way down the front, and triangular facings, akin to robings, run from neckline to hem and fold to the right side of the front opening. The lace-and-faggoting finish runs down the outside edges, is mitered at the bottom and continues to the center front. The remainder of the pelisse is finished in a 3-1/2-inch turned-under, hand-picked hem.

The prettiest detailing and what first catches the eye are the three bows that trim the front opening and conceal the buttons and loops that close the pelisse at these points. The bows are trimmed in Swiss lace and a centered row of featherstitching. Each is caught up at the center with a plain loop of fabric and tacked to the garment.

Misc.9:22/A-1977
Misc.9:22/B-1977

Pink Christening Set

Austrian, 1875-1900

"Perhaps because infants are not in a position clearly to express their disapproval of the way in which they are dressed, the method of clothing them has not received the careful thought and attention which the vital importance of the subject demands."
— From Cradle to School, A Book for Mothers, by the Late Mrs. Ada S. Ballin,
©1902 Constable and Company, London

Nearly everything history maintains about christening apparel and accessories would lead one to dismiss this ensemble from that category of clothing, if it weren't for the fact that the donor who gifted the pieces to the Victoria and Albert Museum of Childhood described the set as a "christening ensemble." It originated in Vienna, Austria, in the late 19th century.

The most noticeable departure from tradition is the color; the underlayer of all three pieces is hot pink silk-backed sateen, which even in its faded state is excruciatingly bright for ceremonial clothing that is traditionally white. Also unusual is the length of what records refer to as "the dress" but what looks more like a bodice or top with a short, sheer organdy skirt or peplum. It begs the question: Is some sort of bloomer or diaper cover missing from the ensemble? Unless the baby were swaddled in the bunting or carrying bed throughout the ceremony, bare legs and plain nappy would have been exposed. Or, the child may have been undressed and totally immersed as part of the ceremony.

Despite the unusual styling, concerted effort went into the construction of all three handmade pieces. The top is a waisted design with a front lace panel comprised of three rows of beading alternating with a diamond-patterned Swiss trim. (The same beading, insertion and edgings are used on all three pieces.) A 1-inch-wide gathered organdy ruffle, trimmed in lace, frames the panel. The neckline is finished in the same gathered ruffle garnished with a triple-tied bow tacked to center front. The whipped and corded seam of the set-in sleeve runs to the front of a piped armscye. The cuff treatment is created from a row of Swiss insertion trimmed on both sides with gathered edging and

topped with a pink bow. The organdy placket is simply turned back 3/4-inch for the length of the garment.

The top fastens on the bodice only with thread-covered buttons and loops leaving the skirt open in back. Casings formed by lines of running stitches are sewn through the outer fabric and lining just above the waistline seam on both back pieces. A long looping drawstring of twill tape is secured at each side seam and is woven through the casings for fitting. The whole of the organdy bodice is lined with hot pink sateen, which is tenuously tailored with rows of hand-stitched tucks so that it fits smoothly into the bodice. The skirt is only 4-3/4-inches long with two 1/8-inch pleats 1/4-inch apart placed 1/2-inch above a 3/8-inch hem. It is completely unlined.

The matching bonnet is quite fancy. The back is a conventional round crown formed with lace beading drawn up tightly into a 1-1/2-inch center circle surrounded with the same lace beading shaped into a second circle. A third organdy circle serves as a base for six 3/4-inch lengths of the beading applied perpendicular to the crown like spokes of a lace pinwheel. The bonnet cap is formed from a 1-1/2-inch-wide strip of organdy joined to a band of beading, Swiss insertion and a second row of beading. The lower edge of the bonnet is finished with a 1-1/4-inch-wide lace ruffle that stops and starts 2-inches into the front opening and folds back to create a double ruffle. One-quarter-inch-long ribbon tabs placed 1-1/2-inches apart encircle the bottom edge, each tacked to the bonnet under the lace edging.

The bunting or carrying bed is a combination of pink silk-backed sateen, organdy and muslin, lined with white cotton and quilting and trimmed with pink ribbons, lace

functional, cotton interior and tied with silk ribbons to the lower corners of the crescent-shaped pillow section. The pillow, where baby's head would have lain, is 8-1/8-inches deep and 16-inches wide. A repeat of the embellished front panel design – the puffing, beading and ruffle – curves around the top and joins to a smaller crescent of organdy. The pillow is layered with a batting or fill and lined with the pink silk-backed sateen.

Misc.128 & A,B-1979
Gift of Mrs. R Bleasdale-Hausmann

Creative Inspiration
Insert tufts of looped ribbon within rows of gathered lace edging for an extra frilly touch.

and beading. The 4-inch pieced bows, tacked at the four corners of the bed front, are made from 2-inch-wide pink satin ribbon. The adorned front consists of six rows of organdy puffing, 1-3/4-inches wide, alternating with five 8-inch rows of beading. Swiss insertion joined to a 2-1/4-inch-wide lace-edged organdy ruffle frames the puffing panel. Strips of beading stripe the ruffle around all four sides, and a second ruffled layer of pinked sateen lends a shadow of color, as does the pink sateen that lines the puffing panel.

The bed contains a removable quilt or mattresslike pad made of cotton. A cotton pocket behind the embellished panel might have held a water bottle for warmth, but it also encases the lower half of the pad. The baby would have been placed on the padded center of the bed, which including the flaps measures 32- x 16- inches. The flaps are approximately 8-inches wide and incorporate four drawstring casings positioned 5-1/2-inches apart. The flaps would have tied together securing the little bundle within, and because the ties gather, they would have drawn up the bed like a cocoon around the baby. The embellished front would have then folded up over the

Silk Puffing and Lace Hood
French, 1900-1920

"Hats and bonnets should be light porous and not too warm. In the summer, large light sunbonnets, with flaps behind should always be worn; and boys' heads and necks should be equally well protected."
— *From Cradle to School, A Book for Mothers*, by the Late Mrs. Ada S. Ballin,
©1902 Constable and Company, London

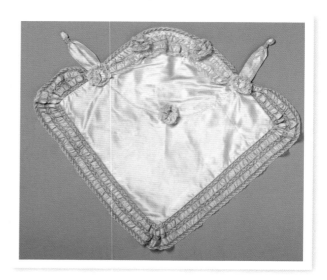

The burnous originated as a hooded cloak worn by Arabs and Moors, and it evolved into a fashionable outer wrap for women worn in the mid-19th century. It was stylized for feminine wear so that it draped around the shoulders like a shawl and tapered into a V at center back. This silk-satin hood with puffing and lace is a miniaturized burnous for a baby. It is lined with cotton flannel and plainly constructed—a triangular "shawl" piece seamed to an elliptical "hood" section. Parallel lines of stitching follow the curved seams, piercing through both layers to create a casing, which when run with satin ribbon serves to draw up the burnous around baby's head. A second casing for a ribbon pull is formed with a bias silk band on the lining side and follows the curved shape of the hood in front. A decorative strip of narrow puffing trimmed with slightly gathered lace edging tops the hood section and is applied in a mirror image to the front curve. The triangular shawl

is trimmed with two strips of lace insertion alternating with narrow strips of puffing, and the entire burnous is framed in a single row of lace edging. Five silk and ribbon rosettes dot the head covering -- to left and right of center front, at the back of the neck, and on each side at the chin line. These latter two rosettes top wide silk ribbon tabs; each is about 2-inches long and knotted at the ends.

Misc.27-1985
Gift of Miss L.E. Willis

Creative Inspiration
Use the idea of pretty double rows of lace and puffing around an elegant bed cover and pillow and monogram it for baby's nursery.

Princess Marina of Greece Dress

Greek, 1910

"Her frocks of lace, her wee jewelled bangles and pins, and her fairy-tale slippers are worthy of a Princess of the blood royal, as of course the small owner is."

— *"London Babies," Town & Country Life, September 3, 1910*

Princess Marina, wife of Prince George, Duke of Kent, was the last foreign-born princess to marry into the British royal family. According to museum records, baby Marina was born in 1906, the youngest daughter of Prince Nicholas and Princess Helen of Greece. She wore this off-white linen dress in 1910 when she was 4 years old, and it is one of just a few garments of royalty held by the V&A Museum of Childhood.

The dress is built around a round yoke of tucked lawn. The neckline is finished in a tiny entredeux and French edging, the yoke line traced in a 2-inch-wide hand-embroidered insertion of a stylized ivy design on linen. The cuffs on the short, puffed sleeves are cut from the same insertion and finished with the neckline lace. The fullness of the dress falls from the yoke in partially stitched box and pencil pleats, stitched down 5-inches into the skirt. The box pleats are 2-1/4-inches wide; the pencil pleats are 3/8-inch wide spaced 1/8-inch apart. The box pleats are ornamented with white frogging – six strips of braid mimicking buttonholes, each topped with a linen-covered shank button and a braided flower. The back of the dress is folded into 20 pencil pleats each 3/8-inch wide; the three pleats to the right of center are incorporated into the placket. The back is secured with three, flat linen-covered buttons and loops visible on the yoke and four additional covered buttons and buttonholes hidden within the placket. The hem is 1-1/2-inches wide and stitched by hand. The circumference of the dress at the hem is 75-inches.

Misc.348-1983
Gift of Mrs. Margaret Langston

Creative Inspiration

Use pretty pleats in three different widths for an economical embellishment. Lend the polish of uniform regalia to the widest of the pleats, fashioning narrow cord into faux buttonholes to pair with self-covered buttons.

Greek Key Lace Dress
English, 1909

"Silk being the fashionable fabric of the season, as well as being reasonable in price on account of the large stocks held by manufacturers, is in demand for young girls' costumes."
— "Modes for Children," *Myra's Journal of Dress and Fashion,* September 1, 1886

Creamy laces in a Greek key design are a distinguishing note in a silk yoke dress for an older child. The "key" pattern originated in Grecian art and design as early as 500 B.C. and has been used on decorative bands ever since. Neoclassic-inspired periods in fashion would revive the motif for use on apparel throughout the 19th and 20th centuries, and these laces are a prime example. Both the insertion and matching edging are 1-1/2-inches wide and interweave the serpentine Greek key with a daisy and leaf vine.

The skirt amounts to a long fancy band finished in a double ruffle. The first section of the fancy band is a 5-inch width of silk with three 1/8-inch tucks worked at the bottom. Following are three lace insertion bands alternating with narrower sections of tucked silk. Between the last row of lace and tucked silk is a double entredeux, presumably to reinforce the seam where it would have borne the weight of the final tier — a ruffle of tucked silk and edging layered over an unadorned, gathered panel of silk with an identical finish. An underlayer of plain silk, finished in a deep hand-picked hem, is incorporated into the entredeux seam and serves to line and puff out the ruffles.

Three 7-inch strips of Greek key insertion lace run from the shoulder seam down the sleeve, each finished in a miter and alternating with rows of three narrow released tucks. The fullness is gathered into a lace cuff trimmed with entredeux-like faggoting run with silk ribbon and gathered lace edging. The portrait collar is shaped to a V in front and fashioned from strips of vertically set lace insertion alternating with 5/8-inch-wide strips of silk topped with a variation on a featherstitch. The collar is outlined in double entredeux mitered at the corners and finished with a gathered, lace-trimmed silk ruffle run with three tucks. The placement of the laces on the collar creates a chevron effect in back. Four loops and buttons are worked into both the dress and collar layers on the placket. The neckline is finished with the same beading used on the cuff and a slightly gathered 1/2-inch edging. The laces and fabric strips throughout the garments are hand-whipped together. Where the lace joins the entredeux, the seams are bound on the inside with silk. The dress is 28-inches long from the back neck.

This piece was made by nuns for the donor, Kathleen Leary, as a child. She remembered wearing it under somber circumstances for her father's funeral, on that occasion with a black sash tied around her waist.

T.861-1974
Gift of Miss Kathleen Leary

Lucy's Party Dress

English, 1890

"A boy's will is the wind's will, according to the poet's song but the girl's will—ah! How different it is! How soft and compliant, how yielding to all outward pressure, how susceptible to the sweet influences of mother-love, how docile and tractable!"
— *Our Manners and Social Customs*, by Daphne Dale,
©1891 Elliott & Beezley Chicago and Philadelphia

The beauty of this piece, aside from the complex construction, is in a small paper tag stitched to the back of the dress. It clearly documents the origin: "Lucy (Ainsworth) Winifred's Party Dress. Worn to a party of the Spears (Lady Lovell is the daughter of Daisy Spears)." Miss Lucy, mother of the donor, was born in Bath in 1884; she wore the dress when she was 6 years old. Making sure to document sewing assures that a special garment won't become a curiosity to future generations.

The front of the dress is formed of a round-necked, cross-shaped center panel in a design that appears to hold in place the pleated side panels. The center is tucked at the sides, and the cross sections are overlapped with pointed side tabs (each tab makes up the top part of a flag-shaped panel; it runs down the side seam, measures 5/8-inch wide at the narrowest point and expands to 2-1/4-inches at the hem).

The tab edges are finished in 1/4-inch satin trim. Cream chenille embroidery outlines the shape of the tabs in a straight line and a looping frill and fills in the middle with an abstract flower. The flower centers are tightly coiled spirals of cream chenille thread; six more spirals adorn the dress front.

Above the tabs, the side panels are neatly folded from the shoulder into 14 knife pleats. Below the tabs, the side panels release into loose tucks, and the center panel is edged in satin trim. The back of the dress is a less-complicated variation of the front. The single piece is folded into seven pleats at the shoulders and has a center placket that closes with six pearlized buttons, hand-stitched buttonholes and a hook and bar at the neck. Tabs, identical to those on the front, extend from the side seams over six pleats.

The elbow-length, straight sleeves are finished with a row of pleats and are also decorated with spirals of appliquéd cream chenille thread.

The bodice is completely lined with muslin, sewn in one with the garment so that the interior seams are visible; the bottom edge of the lining, which ends at the natural waistline, is unattached and finished by machine with a double hem. The square neck edge is finished with a silk facing. The 2-5/8-inch hem has been pieced with a fabric addition applied at an angle and is secured with a hand running stitch.

Misc.157-1979
Gift of Mrs. B. L. Argles

Classic English Smocked Dress
British, 1890-1910

"Many of the costumes are quaint and pretty, especially when they are not too much exaggerated, and one in particular is so simple that it is worth adopting in England, where plain styles are generally preferred for children."

— "Modes for Children," *Myra's Journal*, August 1, 1888

The characteristics of this classic smocked dress are entirely those of the aesthetic movement, which took place in the latter part of 19th-century Britain. Loosely defined, the movement in fashion, art, literature and design was a return to natural production in response to a dislike for crude, machine-made goods and the excesses of Victorian trimmings. In fashion, the lines were less structured with larger sleeves, the fibers natural and the work by hand. This pretty little silk dress meets all three criteria.

English smocking is worked in ivory silk floss and dropped 2-inches below the yoke line on the skirt. It creates a shirred panel, slightly hidden by the collar in front, and manipulates the skirt fullness into a lovely focal point. The smocking in front covers 13 half rows; in back, the abbreviated design covers six. An additional band of smocking at the wrist serves as the cuff and fashions the full sleeve into a Bishop style. Tone-on-tone silk embroidery around the collar is a sweet and subtle complement to the smocking. It creates a frame around the edge with a triple featherstitch and anchors at the front inside corners, with a satin stitch flower and leaves with featherstitched stem and details.

The back placket does not overlap but meets at the center. It is secured by a single loop and flat pearl button at the neck and two additional pairs of buttons, one at the yoke seam and the second 2-inches into the skirt. The right button of the pair is stitched over a thread loop that fastens to the adjacent button. The dress yoke is lined with white cotton twill. Up-close examination of the hemline reveals trails of needle holes that correspond to three growth tucks, which were let out as the child grew. The existing machine-stitched hem is 3 inches deep, and the dress length in its current condition is 28-3/4-inches long.

Misc.718-1992
Gift of Isabella Henrietta Granger

> **Creative Inspiration**
> *Reproduce a timeless design as pretty as the original, using a high yoke pattern and classic English smocking.*

Medallion Yoke Gown

British, 1910-20

"According to my system no change is necessary till the child begins to "feel its feet," and even then, if the clothes are large enough in the body, they may easily be modified so as to be suitable to new conditions by joining the blanket up so as to convert it into a "slip" or princess petticoat, and by putting a tuck in it and in the robe, so that both may just reach the child's ankles."
— From Cradle to School, A Book for Mothers, by the Late Mrs. Ada A. Ballin,
©1902 Constable and Company, London

An original combination of trims and detailing can turn an ordinary high-yoke pattern into something completely unique. Take away the Swiss galloon and this dress becomes just another white baby gown. Galloon is a decorative lace usually with scalloping on both edges; today, it is largely used in lingerie and bridal design. Here, pieces of galloon embroidered around a medallion motif serve a functional purpose, filling in the bulk of the front and back yokes. The shoulder areas of the yoke are cut from white lawn and folded into two sections of five 1/8-inch tucks. The compound scalloped edges of the galloon are applied in a hand picked seam over the top of the finished edges of the shoulder fabric and the gathered skirt fabric.

The skirt is embellished with two strips of faggoting in an entredeux-like design that coordinates nicely with the galloon but was unlikely created to do so. The bottom is finished in conventional hem turned under 1/4-inch then 1-1/2-inches, but finished in an unconventional way: French knots trail around the skirt, decorating and securing the hem at the same time.

The neckline is finished in a tiny casing run with pink embroidery floss and topped with gathered French lace edging. The long sleeves end in the same gathered edging. A 1/2-inch ecru satin ribbon secured at each sleeve seam would have tied around baby's wrist, gathering in the sleeve fullness and forming a ruffled finish over the little one's hands. The same ribbon runs through the faggoting in the skirt. A button-and-loop closure joins the yoke together at the stress point just above the skirt seam. The dress is 24-inches long, and the skirt circumference is 64-inches.

B.584-1993
Gift of Miss Eileen A. Brock

Candy Cane Dress
Anglo-Indian, 1900-1925

"The child's world is, however, at the largest a little one, and it is necessary to enlarge it by various means, including stories and pictures, songs and books."
— "The Teaching of English," by J.C Stobart from the *London Mercury*, republished in *The Living Age*, January 10, 1920

Indian or chikan embroidery was a less expensive substitute for authentic Ayrshire embroidery or Valenciennes laces and became increasingly more prevalent as the Ayrshire industry dissolved. Examples of Indian origin like this muslin baby dress are typically made of coarser materials, and the decorative work is less precise. Although records indicate this piece was made some time in the early 1900s, its styling emulates that of a mid-1800s gown with some earlier detailing. For example, the scalloped robings curve gracefully from around the neckline of the dress to the hem and face outward; such

placement is indicative of the romantic period. The princess-line silhouette common to christening gowns throughout the 1800s is emphasized by the triangular skirt panel and V-shaped bodice panel. This could indicate that a much longer dress was "short-coated" for a crawling baby. The dresses which were shortened at this date were often taken apart at the waist to preserve the decorative hem finishes; the embroidery design is identical to that of the skirt robings; if it were altered, the seamstress who did so preserved the original design elements.

The focal point of the skirt embroidery is an interlocking candy-cane motif worked in an Indian drawn-thread filling. It is outlined with a framework of stem stitch and running stitch and surrounded by whitework in a nonspecific vinelike design. Similar embroidery fills in the bodice panel around a less-elaborate flower motif.

The waistline and scooped neckline are finished with casings and drawstring closures. The application of the short raglan sleeve includes baby piping both at the armscye and at the seam of the embroidered edging. The dress is 23-inches long, and the skirt circumference is 74-inches.

Misc.664-1991
Gift of Miss Barbara Watson

Creative Inspiration
Fashion a holiday reproduction of the Indian drawn-thread filling by shaping a wide lace insertion into a similar candy-cane motif.

Medley of Embroidery Dress

English, 1915

"The embroideries are in appearance equal to the best Scotch and Swiss work, although they do not rival the Madeira work. They are made in edgings and insertions with and without a hemstitch finish, and are sold at most moderate prices, from two shillings the piece."
— Editorial, *Myra's Journal of Dress and Fashion*, January 1, 1876

A family heirloom in the truest sense, this dress was made for Caroline Constance, the eldest child of Dr. and Mrs. Andreae and later worn by her six sisters, Mary, Janet, Elizabeth, Bridget, Philippa and Octavia, as well as their brother John. It is a baby dress, and since Caroline was born in June 1915, according to museum records, it is safe to assume it was made in that year or shortly thereafter. The family members listed in the records resided in London and throughout the English countryside at the time the dress was gifted to the museum in 1981.

The dress is white batiste or English muslin, and the bodice is lined with cotton netting. The skirt fabric appears to be Indian Ayrshire, which is noticeably coarser than authentic Ayrshire, and it is embroidered all over in white silk worked in floral sprigs. The bodice is a midwaist style decorated with tucks and elaborate whitework embroidery fashioned into a V. It was built around a mitered center section of openwork insertion

joined to the embroidered fabric with a tiny faggoting stitch that at first glance could be mistaken for entredeux. A pale pink silk ribbon embroidered with rosebuds runs through the beading or ribbon slot that serves to bridge the bodice to the skirt and finishes the sleeves. The sleeve beading is edged with a gathered French lace that is also whipped to the neckline. Vertical rows of openwork insertion traverse the front, sides and back of the skirt and are joined to the skirt panels with entredeux. Two rows of the insertion meet at center front and back and are joined with a faggoting stitch. Entredeux reinforces the seam at the armscye. A wrist casing inside the sleeves is run with pink ribbon that draws up the sleeve fullness and ties into a bow. The dress is 23-1/2-inches long with a circumference of 56-inches. A 2-inch frill at the hem is a deep section of embroidered edging applied with entredeux. The back is fastened with a drawstring tape at the neck, the slotted ribbon at the waist and one small pearlized button. A few areas of wear and repair are to be expected in a garment handed down to so many children.

Misc.285-1981
Gift of Mrs. Mary Webb, Mrs. Janet Grimm, Mrs. Elizabeth Everington, Miss Philippa Andreae and Mrs. Octavia O'Reilly

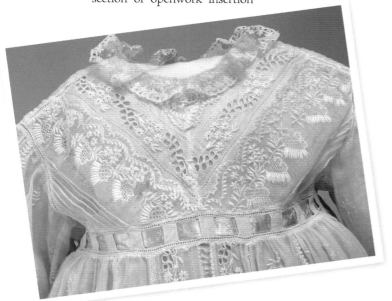

Creative Inspiration

Sometimes the sheer beauty of a design is in the lack of contrivance. Make use of lace bits and pieces by combining them into a special dress for an original and economical approach to heirloom sewing.

Floral Sprays and Scallops Dress
British, 1914-1920

"I long for the baby to wander hither to me
Like a wind-shadow wandering over the water,
So that she can stand on my knee
With her little bare feet in my hands,
Cool like syringa buds,
Firm and silken like pink young peony flowers."

— Excerpt from "A Baby Running Barefoot" by D.H. Lawrence

Making do with the materials at hand is the mantra of the home seamstress and quite likely the provenance of this simple, waisted baby dress. It is a combination of handwork (the bodice) and pre-embroidered yardage (the skirt), which is believed to have been drapery or women's blouse fabric very probably obtained by someone who worked in a factory that used or manufactured clothing or yard goods. The machine embroidery design on the skirt is a floral spray repeat. A second row of smaller single daisy sprays repeats 1-inch above the border work, and a third row of even smaller daisy sprays repeats 1-inch above that. Although these smaller motifs are uniformly stitched into the batiste ground, they appear to be tossed randomly as the result of the fabric being gathered into the waistband. The prettiest part of the machine work is the compound scallop at the hem of the skirt. A tiny double row of satin stitching finishes the very edge, and a single daisy is embroidered within each scallop.

The embroidery motifs on the bodice are rather crudely stitched and resemble 18th-century goffering patterns, presumably designed to complement the machine work on the skirt, pulling out the daisies and similar greenery. It is worked on an insert whipped into the center front of the dress and framed with a row of satin-stitch dots. Five tiny pintucks, 1/8-inch apart, are worked on each side of the insert just below the neckline and range from 2- to 3-inches long. A sprig of embroidered greenery is tossed at the shoulder, and a single daisy and curve of four eyelets are worked at the sides of the bodice. The 3/4-length sleeves are finished with a turned-back cuff, scalloped on the edge in a chain stitch and embroidered with a single daisy. The neckline is finished in bias casing and drawstring with a 1/4-inch-wide straight lace edging applied below the casing. The placket in back is 10-1/2-inches long. The dress is secured at the neck with a drawstring, and a single button and buttonhole are positioned midway down the placket.

The dress measures 22-inches from center front. The skirt is joined to the bodice with an entredeux-edged bridging in an art deco-esque design of overlapping ovals with tiny squares at the centers. The dress is completely hand sewn. All the seams are French inside except for the raw armscye seams.

Misc.771-1986
Gift of Mrs. C.
Fawcett

Double-Puffed Sleeve Dress

English, 1825-1930

"Perhaps no subject has occupied more attention than dress. It is an end which we propose in almost all our labours. Dress has stimulated ingenuity to the greatest variety of inventions. The vanity of the world keeps the world in emotion. Dress spreads the sail and opens the furrow. Dress is the pride of the infant on the lap, and the overgrown child of thirty. Dress is the darling toy of the fair and the chief accomplishment of the soldier. It calls into exercise the taste of mankind. Take away dress, and the polished circles would have not subject for criticism. The beauties of the age would sink into lifeless indifference…In writing on dress, it is necessary to proceed with caution. The manufacturer, the merchant, the statesman — all are interested in this weighty subject. Dress influences the cabinet of policy as well as the toilet of beauty. The prosperity of nations is connected with a passion for dress. England could not have fought in her battles without her broadcloths, nor France have enchained nations without her laces."

— "The Importance of Dress," *The Juvenile Port – Folio, and Literary Miscellany*, July 6, 1816

Noreen Marshall, curator of Dress, Doll and Childcare Collections at the V&A Museum of Childhood, is almost certain that this white English lawn dress was originally a much longer dress, which was shortened to its current state. The family or seamstress would have referred to this practice as "short-coating," and it originally occurred around the time a baby began to toddle – about 12 months in the 18th century, but gradually lessening to a few months in the 19th and dying out in the 20th because the very long clothes were discontinued. However, nothing indicates whether the dress was shortened for the original baby who wore it or by someone who perhaps inherited it generations later. What can be assumed is that to salvage the elegant hem embellishment, the length wasn't cut from the bottom. Instead, the skirt was most likely detached and several feet cut from the top before re-attaching it at the waistline. Even more intriguing than how or when it was shortened to its current state is the sleeve treatment; the puffed design is actually a double puff applied to a triangular shoulder yoke. One thing this construction does is form the neck squarer because the yoke makes a straight edge over the shoulder. The sleeves are attached with French seams and are finished with a bias binding topped with tiny French knots and a narrow Ayrshire edging.

The embellishment throughout is an elaborate use of needlepoint filling typical of Ayrshire embroidery. The work is densely fashioned on the bodice, shoulder yokes, robings and around the hemline where it is interwoven with whitework and eyelets. A single floral motif is repeated on the skirt, growing ever so slightly larger toward the hemline and each time worked with one of five different needlepoint fillings.

The waistband incorporates two casings, at the top and the bottom, so when pulled to fit, the effect would be a puffed or ruched waistline. A drawstring and casing also serve to fit the dress at the scooped neckline. The dress is entirely handmade.

T.40-1966
Gift of Mrs. Miles Swanston

Creative Inspiration

Practically a lost art, Ayrshire created some of the most magnificent handwork to date. Achieve a look similar to the time-consuming craft by working a small satin-stitch appliquéd shape over a piece of lace, carefully trimming fabric from behind and framing the appliqué with delicate whitework embroidery.

Plum Silk Coat Dress
English, 1820-1830

*"When she was a baby, in her mother's arms, she was very sweet and good-natured
indeed; and if you could have seen how her father and mother fondled and caressed her,
you would have said, 'I don't believe Jane will ever love to eat sugar-plums better
than her father and mother like to kiss her.'"*
— "Little Jane," *The Juvenile Miscellany*, May 1830

This little girl's silk coat dress is nearly 200 years old. The trim on the bodice has the influence of Hussar (Hungarian for "bandits") regiment dress uniforms, which were immensely fancy. The front is trimmed with braids in graduated widths stitched down with covered buttons. This same braid trim outlines the shape of the collar, the V-shaped bodice overlay, skirt overlap, sash and lower edges of the sleeves. A faux cuff or wrist frill is fashioned by a silk band folded into a single-loop bow and tacked to the top of the sleeve; it winds around the wrist and fastens with a loop to a fabric-covered button. The loop is made from the narrow braid, which also trims the band. The sash is tacked to the center front just under the bodice overlay and fits the garment around the waist, drawing in the fullness and forming a large elegant bow in back. The straight skirt is a wrap style that overlaps in front. The dress is ankle length with wrist-length sleeves and was handmade in England between 1820 and 1830. It is lined in white silk and is in remarkable condition, considering the fragility of the fabric.

T.103-1932
Gift of Miss Burke-Wood

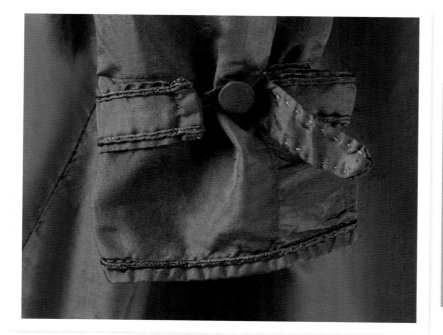

Creative Inspiration
*Gather a straight sleeve on a coat or
robe for a comfortable fit simply by
topping the sleeve at the wrist with
a narrow self-band (applied in the
underarm seam) and a loop and
button fastening.*

Flowering Vine Conversion Dress
British, 1860-1869

"It seems sometimes as if economy were the chief object kept in view by those whose occupation it is to design new costumes for children, for the new modes strike one at the first glance as being full of suggestions for the alteration of old dresses, and of possible economies, which may help to add another season to the existence of costumes that have been put aside as not worth the trouble and expense of doing up again."
— "Modes for Children," *Myra's Journal of Dress and Fashion*, October 1, 1886

This fine white linen piece was noticeably inspired by historic dress, as it was originally made in the mid-19th century but speaks to a much earlier 16th-century garb. The style demonstrates the construction of a dress with a kirtle and farthingale. In the 16th century, the kirtle is the dress — a joined bodice and skirt — and the farthingale is the underskirt. An authentic farthingale fashioned between about 1545 and 1620 would have been more like a stiffened petticoat. The facsimile on

this garment, a cotton underskirt, is embellished around the hem with three sections of 1/4-inch-wide tucks and a fancy lace band. Centered in front is a rhombus-shaped lace insert made of 3/4-inch-wide diagonally placed insertion, flanked at the sides with the same insertion and finished at the top and bottom with 1-3/4-inch-wide insertion. The cheat is that when the overskirt hangs in its natural position, this lacework on the farthingale appears to run the circumference of the skirt like the tucks and fancy band. In truth, it was designed solely to fill in the front skirt opening, an economical approach that conserves lace that would otherwise be hidden beneath the overskirt.

Someone went back to the bits bag and fished out more of the narrower lace insertion to raise the draw-cord neckline, which in its original state was cut quite low. The dress was converted, probably for another generation, by creating a higher, more rounded neckline finished with a gathered lace edging and adding a long, slightly puffed sleeve underneath the original lace-edged, split-capped sleeve.

The narrow lace insertion is an eyelet and foliage pattern in an Ayrshire-like technique. The wider edging is of a repeating floral motif and intertwining vine. French-lace edging finishes both original and new necklines. A French insertion embellishes the sleeve cuff.

The bodice has a V-shaped panel at the center front, a representation of the earlier basque waist, and is composed of horizontally aligned insertion joined to angled strips of floral insertion on either side and finished

with French-lace edging. The bodice back is finished with two pairs of partly stitched vertical tucks and the waist, with a single row of speckle stitch, a very popular stitch in England during the 16th century, so adding to the Elizabethan appearance. The gathered, slightly shorter overskirt is finished at the hem and edges with parallel tucking, mitered floral insertion and French edging. The garment fastens at the back of the bodice with waist and neck drawstrings, a button and stitched buttonhole, and a button and loop.

This gown is said to have been worn by the donor's grandmother Maud Kathleen Sinclair (born in the 1860s) and the donor's mother, Moira Clover Brown (born October 23, 1905). The length of the overskirt is 16-inches. The total back length of the gown is 29-1/2-inches.

Misc.1025-1992
Gift of Miss R. Maxwell

Creative Inspiration

For heirloom designs with a skirt overlay, save on lace by smartly making the lace treatment on the skirt only wide enough to fill in the front opening. There's no need to embellish where work is hidden beneath another fabric layer.

Eyelet Wisteria Dress
English, 1910-1920

"H. Walker's Needles.
The 'QUEEN'S OWN' WITH LARGE EYES AND Patent ridges, to facilitate sewing are
the best for every kind of needlework. Those who have once used them will use no others.
53 Gresham Street, London
— Advertisement, Myra's Journal of Dress and Fashion, *November 1, 1879*

The origin of this linen christening gown is listed as English, but it serves as an exquisite example of hand embroidery, which was quite possibly rendered in Switzerland. On the skirt panel, a graduating wisteria design spills into an elaborate eyelet and Battenberg vessellike motif that follows the inset's triangular shape. The embroidery starts 28-inches into the skirt with a single, small eyelet wisteria. The floral work increases in size to midway down the skirt, where it meets the triangular design of round eyelet rows alternating with rows of openwork filled with single-strand featherstitching and rows of satin-stitched dots. The bodice V is a frame of floral-shaped eyelets around a stylized eyelet design with a touch of satin-stitched leaves and what looks like a cluster of gooseberries. The point of the inset extends over the narrow waistband casing that is topped with a line of featherstitching. The loose point is designed to be tucked in at a small waist opening when worn by a girl, or, as with this dress, the opening is tacked closed and the point left out for a boy.

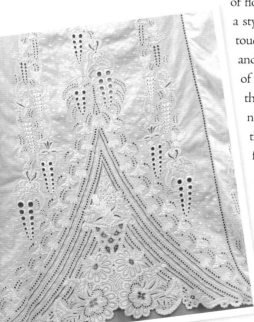

Graduated robings, finished along the edge with sharp scalloping and eyelets, outline the bodice inset and skirt panel. The skirt robings are 1-inch wide at the waist and widen to 2-3/4-inches at the bottom. The same scalloped edge, trimmed to 1/2-inch wide, finishes the neckline in front. In back it widens to 1-1/2-inches where it edges the collar pieces and completes the back part of the neckline casing.

The interior seams on the bodice are French as are the side seams of the skirt. The interior waistline seam of the skirt is turned back, and the 1/4-inch seam allowance is left raw. There is a purpose to leaving an unfinished seam at the waist; it would have made it simpler to shorten the gown if desired by taking out the waist seam and pulling the skirt upward, thereby salvaging the extraordinary work at the bottom. The whole of the gown is 40-1/2-inches long from the front neckline to the hemline.

Circ.216-1930
Gift of Mr. H. E. Clarke Hutton

Creative Inspiration
Pay tribute to classic christening tradition by incorporating a center front point extension into the bodice embellishment. For a baby boy, the tab is worn out, and for a girl, it tucks into a slit in the bodice-to-skirt seam.

Sixty-five Tucks Dress
United Kingdom, 1870

"Little babies, you know, cannot undress themselves and put themselves to bed; but their mothers, or their nurse, does it for them and then stays by them until they get fast asleep, for fear that they should fall out of bed."
— "Little Jane," *The Juvenile Miscellany*, May 1830

It's tempting to manufacture a history for vintage pieces that have survived the ages with no story of their own. This one uses tucks as the primary embellishment, 65 to be exact, filling in the center panel of the skirt; each one is folded to a precise 1/8-inch and hand-stitched. Did the number 65 hold some significance? Could the gown have been made in 1865? Trying to unravel the origins of these garments, however fruitless at times, is part of the fascination of the study.

What is clear is that the dress was constructed by hand from the first stitch to the last but incorporates machine-crafted Swiss trims or broderie anglaise into the design. Swiss embroideries were machine produced from about 1870 onward, according to Pat Earnshaw's book *A Dictionary of Lace* (Dover Publications). This solves at least one mystery: This gown in its entirety couldn't have been made in 1865. The bodice edging and insertion are tied together through common fernlike embroidery worked as fill around eyelet flowers. The bodice V is formed with five strips of insertion, one centered straight up and down, two set at slight angles on the sides, and wedges alternating between. Each strip is joined to the next with hand featherstitching applied to the turned-under selvedge. Robings of Swiss embroidered edging trim the sides of the bodice, running from the waist seam, up over the shoulder and around to the back placket. A casing run with a draw cord, topped with featherstitching and edged in a slightly gathered 1/2-inch-wide French lace completes the neckline. The bodice-to-skirt seam is concealed by an identical casing minus the French lace. The cap sleeves are cut entirely from the same Swiss edging used for the robings. The back bodice is unadorned except for four vertical tucks, two folded at each side of the simple placket. A single button and buttonhole secure the placket at the center, working in tandem with the drawstrings at the neck and waist.

The tucked skirt panel is divided down the center with a strip of Swiss insertion, a coordinate to the bodice insertion, trimmed at the sides with a second Swiss edging that is similar in feel to the bodice edging but of a different design. The same lace composition runs down the sides of the panel to extend the robing effect from the bodice. The laces run the length of the skirt where they are mitered into a pretty tab finish over the plain 2-inch-wide hem. The total back length of the gown is 40-1/2- inches; the circumference is 74-inches.

Circ.1073-1924
Gift of Miss B. M. Cunnington

Curiosity Gown

English, 1850-1860 and 1890-1900

"On this special occasion there was a charming little bit of news to discuss over the cups; a messenger had arrived during our absence, from the residence of the married son of our host, to announce the birth of a daughter, and the ceremonies attendant on the entrance of a baby into this busy world were talked over and anticipated."
— "Chateau Life in England," *Littell's Living Age*, April 13, 1850

Several design elements on this gown support the earlier date of origin. The scooped décolletage, drawstring closures at the waist and neckline, V-shaped bodice, and robings and capped sleeves cut from Swiss edging are all typical of mid-19th-century styling. Also telling is the way the Swiss insertions are joined together – with hand featherstitching applied to the turned-under selvedge – and the use of additional featherstitching down the robings and on top of the casings.

The skirt, however, gives a clothing historian pause. It is cut from pre-embroidered yardage that was likely manufactured closer to the turn of the century. It is a chain-stitched design of a single bow and miscellaneous flowers that pour into a modernistic scalloped design around the hem, quite possibly a product of the art nouveau movement. Still, the muslin fabric of the bodice and skirt are virtually identical, which might suggest that both pieces were constructed and assembled at the same time, perhaps as late as 1890 or 1900. An assumption could be made that an older person, a grandmother or a great-aunt, used modern materials but made an elegant gown using a style familiar to her rather than heeding the current mode of dress. A third possibility, suggested by robings on the bodice but not the skirt, is that it may be a combination of two gowns the family had.

The original catalog record from 1963 states that Miss Joan Hassall, the illustrator, gave it to the museum and that the Baden-Powell family had given it to her mother. Robert Baden-Powell, the founder of the Scouting movement, and Miss Hassall's father, illustrator John Hassall, were both members of the London Sketch Club.

Additional facts are that the length from the center back is 41-3/4-inches and the circumference at the hem is 67-1/2-inches.

T. 227-1963
Gift of Miss Joan Hassall

Cameo Rose Gown

English, 1923

"You must read it. Every one else is reading it. London devoured four editions in a month. And every one who loves children shouldn't let this bit of child literature go by. The Young Visiters comes in a funny little edition 'compleat' with a photograph of the author and a reproduction of a page of the stout two-penny notebook to which it was confided in pencil and where it has lain these many years."

— "The Young Visiters," The Independent, January 31, 1920

This gown's bodice, formed of two pieces of wide Swiss edging, exemplifies the inherent ingenuity of the seamstress. The two pieces of Swiss are butted together along the scalloped-edge finish, forming an elegant midyoke with embroidery interest. The scalloped join is aligned at the yoke center and is backed with a strip of plain white cotton, which fills in what would otherwise be open areas between the scallops. The neckline is finished in a bias casing that houses a draw cord to fit the dress to the child's form.

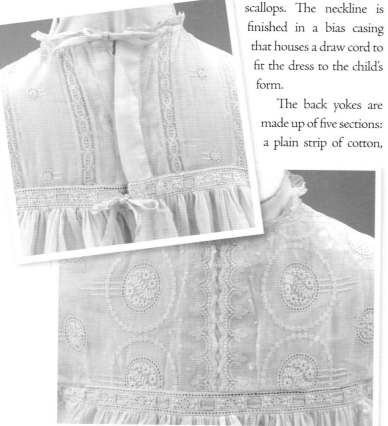

The back yokes are made up of five sections: a plain strip of cotton, two strips of 5/8-inch-wide French lace insertion that flank a strip of Swiss fabric sparingly embroidered with only two small eyeletlike flowers, and finally a second strip of cotton cut from the selvedge and turned back to form a placket that closes with two fabric-covered buttons. Both front and back yokes are stitched at the waist to a pretty Swiss beading, which is run with an ecru ribbon that ties the garment together in back. The long set-in sleeves are finished in entredeux beading, a narrow muslin cuff and a tiny French lace edging.

The skirt is a deep cut of Swiss embroidery; the primary design is a repeating motif of cameo roses above a pretty serpentine scalloped edge. The design blends aptly with the bodice embroidery, although the laces are clearly different patterns. Mixing lace patterns is an accepted part of the art of what has come to be known as heirloom sewing. It can be the result of having limited resources; it can be an indication that something was pieced together from separate garments; or it can be an intentional choice, an expression of creativity and a stamp of individuality. This particular gown is one of a collection of pieces that came from a donor whose mother was a professional with access to unusual fabrics; she worked in the clothing industry as a "sample hand" making up women's blouses.

The back dress length on this piece is 29-inches. The circumference of the skirt is 60-inches. The interior seams are French, and the sewing was done by machine.

Misc.75(6)-1976
Gift of Miss Renee Weller

Rows of Flowers Gown
British, 1896-1906

"To Mothers! Woodward's 'Gripe Water' or Infants' preservative is the only really safe remedy
for all disorders of Infants and Children especially for difficult teething.
From Miss Emily Faithful. – 'This medicine has been found most beneficial in the various
disorders attending baby life. It is so simple a remedy that Mothers need not fear to use it.'
London Dept: Messrs. Sanger, 489, Oxford St."
— "Needlework," *Macmillin's Magazine* reprinted in *Littell's Living Age*, November 1, 1873

There is nothing particularly intricate about the two machine-made Swiss insertions used on this late 19th-century christening gown, they're just very pretty. One, which is 1-1/4-inches wide, alternates two different flowers, and the other, 7/8-inch wide, repeats a floral vine. Joined together to fill the gown center panels, they create the impression of a neatly sown row garden. The insertions were milled with a drawn-thread border with a batiste seam allowance. Featherstitching worked on top of the turned-back selvedge joins together the insertions. A lovely 2-1/2-inch-wide edging in a fuchsia blossom and eyelet design with a compound scalloped edge is used for the robings that run from the back around the neck and down the whole of the gown. This same edging is used for loosely gathered ruffles that interrupt the insertion rows at

several places down the front panel. The edging was also used to fashion the cap sleeves.

The V-shaped panel on the scooped-neck bodice is defined by the wider of the two insertions and is filled in with alternating rows of both insertions. The neckline is a traditional casing finish, topped with a row of featherstitching and edged with a slightly gathered French lace. The casing application is repeated at the waist, and both are run with draw cords that tie in back. Two laundry marks, "LKZ" in blue thread and "K23" in red thread, are crudely embroidered on the bodice interior.

The front skirt panel is an inverted V shape filled with insertions and flounces. The top section starts with an inch-wide strip of batiste followed by 16 alternating rows of the insertion. The second section is comprised of a single row of insertion between two batiste panels topped with edging ruffles. The third section is five alternating rows of insertion. The fourth and final section is a single row of Swiss insertion between a panel of batiste topped with an edging ruffle and a deep row of gathered edging. All the sections and laces are overlapped and joined with hand featherstitching. Outside the center panel, the skirt is embellished toward the bottom with a 7/8-inch-wide tuck between two sets of four 1/4-inch-wide tucks and finished with a plain 2-1/8-inch-wide hem.

The total back length of the gown is 39-1/2 inches. The circumference is 80-inches.

Misc.69-1988
Gift of Miss Q. E. M. Crapper

Flounced Tiers Gown
United Kingdom, 1850-1860

"If she were less fertile she would be less popular among the masses. The poor Irish or English woman standing before one of the pictures in the Strand, which represents the Queen with the royal babies around her, feels flattered by the reflection that the Queen, after all, has the same propensities, instincts and affections as rule her."
— *"The Queen of England," Home Journal, July 7, 1855*

A mid-19th-century piece, this long baby's gown is atypical compared with the traditional scooped décolletage with drawstring finish, capped sleeves and high or midyoke bodice. It is sized for a baby, yet the to-the-waist silhouette with turn-down collar and elongated, double puffed sleeve is a style historically reserved for an older child.

The fabric is muslin. The trims consist of floral embroidered insertion, an airy eyelet edging, piping and eight thread-covered shank buttons. Where the insertions or edgings interrupt the flow of fabric, the joins are topped with a heavy triple featherstitch. This technique is particularly evident in the bodice decoration – a wedge-shaped central panel is made up of mitered chevron-shaped strips of the floral-embroidered insertion, which has a drawn thread border. The featherstitch is worked between the rows of drawn threadwork emphasizing the chevron line. The buttons form a vertical row down the center front over the mitered seam.

The collar and robings are fashioned from the same materials – unadorned muslin edged in eyelet secured with featherstitching. The unusual sleeve is gathered onto a cord at the center creating the double-puffed effect.

The skirt is cartridge-pleated to the bodice, and the waistband casing is trimmed with eyelet edging and topped with featherstitching. The central panel of the skirt is trimmed with mitered V-shapes of embroidered insertion alternating with scalloped frills. The side robings are edged to match the collar. Robings on many baby gowns are examples of fashion being copied with no understanding of what robings are for or where they came from. Robings were originally used to give women's gowns the effect of a separate coat. Thus they were positioned inward and traveled down the gown. Eventually, however, they became frills and for some reason turned outward, becoming purely decorative. Tucks were logically applied to children's apparel to allow for growth but in time these, too, became decorative like the ones on this gown. The finished back length of the dress is 46-inches. The skirt circumference is 92-inches.

Misc.482-1991
Gift of Henriette Syarauw

Creative Inspiration
There was a time when embroidered handkerchiefs were considered a necessity, and, even today, antiques stores generally have a fine selection. Set several handkerchiefs of coordinating motifs at angles down the front of a skirt panel, place mitered Vs of lace insertion over the seams and trim from behind.

Curved Lace Godet Gown

British, 1900-1904

"After each little gown has had all the stitches put into it, after it is certain that the deft fingers cannot make the garments of the king any more beautiful, then they should be done up in packages and tied with either pink or blue ribbons, while between the garments should be tiny linen sachets filled with orris root and having their ends fringed."
— "The Baby's Layette," by Isabel A. Mallon, *The Ladies' Home Journal*, October 1892

Records reveal that the donor, Helen Grimshaw, wore this garment at her christening at St. Saviour's Church St. Georges Square, Pimlico, in August 1904. She believed that the gown may also have been used for the baptism of her elder brother, Nicholas O'Donell Grimshaw, who was born in December 1899 and christened in January at the same church.

With the construction date firmly established, interest turns to the design, which focuses on the decorative center panel. The lacework brings to mind Seminole Patchwork, a quilting technique originally developed by Seminole Indian women in the late 1800s to create larger pieces of cloth from remnants. It is highly unlikely that native Americans inspired the lacework on this christening gown, as it was constructed across the ocean at the time Seminole Patchwork was being developed. However, if the pieced-lace design was the seamstresses' ingenious way of stretching cuts of lace yardage, it does raise a question about the sisterhood of sewing: Did a native American and an English lady, two women from completely different worlds, let a needle and thread guide them to eerily similarly results?

The front of the dress is a princess line filled with a center panel of alternating horizontal strips of 1-1/4-inch-wide Swiss and 1-inch-wide French insertion laces. A slight curve is introduced to the lacework just below the waist, and the curves become more pronounced as the panel widens toward the hem. The laces are featherstitched at the edges, and a single row of Swiss insertion divides the panel vertically down the center. Gores of the same curved and alternating lace pattern, edged vertically on the interior side with the Swiss insertion, are applied at the waist and extend to the bottom ruffle. The Swiss insertion forms the princess line at the sides of the panel while finishing the outer edge of each gore. The panel design continues with a batiste section of seven 1/16-inch tucks spaced 1/8-inch apart, a row of Swiss insertion and four slightly gathered Swiss edging ruffles, establishing a lovely waterfall effect.

Swiss edge robings extend from the back placket over the shoulder, where they butt with the neckline, and follow the princess line to the hem. The join is topped with featherstitching. The gathered wrist-length sleeves have a cuff of Swiss insertion, which is finished in a narrow French edging, as is the scooped neckline. The neckline appears to have been a standard casing design originally, but if so, the casing was at some time stitched up perhaps in a botched repair. On either side of the back placket are five 1/4-inch vertical tucks that run the length of the bodice. Inside, the back bodice has one label with the name "Grimshaw" stitched in red, a family mark, and a second label stitched with "3G7" in black, which would have served as a laundry mark.

The back length of this handmade gown is 42-inches. The bottom width of the front panel is 29-inches. The circumference of the dress is 74-inches. The hem outside the front panel is 3/4-inch deep with an underlay of Swiss edging.

Misc.482-1991
Gift of Henriette Syarauw

Rose Bouquet Conversion Gown
Irish, 1860-1875

"Well, this family of husband and wife was one morning augmented by the arrival of a baby, for which, as I learned in the course of the day, little or no preparation in the way of apparel had been made, and this little stranger was accordingly clothed with such scraps of dress as the young ladies and I could gather together at a short notice – all of which was declared to do beautifully – 'Thank God.' "
— *"A Governess's Recollections of Ireland,"* Saturday Evening Post, June 19, 1850

Although family members believe this gown was made around 1910, its style suggests it may have been made much earlier and altered for the babies who wore it in the 20th century. It was worn by the donor, Mrs. Noreen Hamilton of London, who was born in 1913, her older sister, Diana, born in 1910 and her younger sister, Cecilia, born in 1916, all in Ireland. It is most definitely a conversion gown, as evidenced by the two-part sleeves. The short lace cap is original to the gown, and although the longer elements were added later, these may have been made using vintage fabric of the 1820s or 30s. It is possible that the sleeves were cut from another family heirloom dress and inserted into this gown, since the neckline and cuff laces match. Long sleeves were more fashionable at the time and were considered to be better for keeping the child warm. Overall, the gown is a minimal conversion, with no alteration to the neck, and described in museum records to be "1860-75, with later alterations."

This Irish linen, to-the-waist bodice style has a traditional front panel formed with strips of Swiss insertion and wedges of French lace. The Swiss design of the insertion and matching edging is a series of rose bouquets framed with tiny eyelets. The 1-inch-wide French bobbin lace is a nondescript flower along a serpentine vine. A third French bobbin lace edging has a simple scalloped edge and is slightly gathered at the top of the neckline casing and around the sleeve cuffs. Comprising the front skirt panel are eight sections that consist of a centered strip of Swiss insertion between two batiste strips folded with two 1/4-inch tucks. Each Swiss-to-batiste join, as well as the neck and waist casings, are topped with a double row of tiny French knots. The sections alternate with single rows of the French bobbin lace insertion and finish at the hem with a slightly gathered 2-1/2-inch-wide Swiss edging. The Swiss edging also serves as the robings, which run from the neck back to the front hem.

The skirt outside the center front panel is embellished approximately two-thirds of the way down with five sections of tucks placed 1-1/4-inches apart. The tucks are 1/4-inch-wide and 1/4-inch apart. The final tucked section ends 3/4-inch above a plain 1-1/2-inch-deep hem.

Drawstrings close the gown at the back neckline and waist as do a single button and buttonhole placed midway down the bodice placket. The long puffed sleeves are secured at the cuff with a tiny covered button and a fabric loop. The gown is a product of hand construction, and the back length is 40-inches.

Misc.213-1983
Gift of Mrs. Noreen Hamilton

Plum Lace Gown

English, 1902

"Little Jack Horner
Sat in the corner eating his Christmas pie
He put in his thumb and pulled out a plum
And said, 'What a good boy am I!'"
—Traditional English nursery rhyme, said have been based on events surrounding Henry the VIII and his disbanding of Catholic monasteries and abbeys in England in the 1530s and 40s.

This beautiful silk christening gown melds three different nations; the fabric is Japanese, the lace is thought to be European and the gown is thought to have been constructed in England, where the babies who wore it were christened. Both the donor, Mrs. E.M. (Hoe) Rowbotham, and her brother Edgar were christened in the gown in West Dulwich; she was born in 1902 and he, in 1906.

The use of a lace with a plum motif in combination with a Japanese silk could be serendipitous, but it could also be by design. Nature is a rich source of kimono motifs, and the plum, the first tree to blossom each year, is considered a symbol of renewal. Relevance to a christening ceremony is thus conceivable.

The gown design is a basic yoke, not unlike classic dresses still made in the heirloom tradition. The yoke consists of alternating vertical strips of featherstitched self bands and plum lace and is framed with a gathered plum lace edging. The neckline is a bias band topped with featherstitching and floral French edging that does not match but blends nicely with the plum lace. The same lace edges the long bishop sleeves beneath two 1/2-inch-wide rows of ruching that suggest a separate cuff.

The skirt is plain silk for approximately 15-inches where it meets seven rows of horizontal plum lace insertion alternating with six featherstitched self bands of silk. The hem finish is a double flounce of the plum edging; the first flounce is the same 2-inch-wide lace that frames the bodice gathered over a band of silk, and the second ruffle is a 3-1/2-inch-wide matching plum lace edging joined to the silk band.

The garment fastens in back with a ribbon drawstring at the neck and has two pearlized buttons with stitched buttonholes. The lace is machine made. A tag is stitched in the back bodice of this dress embroidered with the name "Rowbotham," a family mark. The back length of the dress is 40-inches.

Misc.206-1983
Gift of Mrs. E. M. Rowbotham

Dainty Triple Scallops Gown

English, 1916 -1917

"Today I saw a little calm-eyed child –
Where soft lights rippled and the shadows tarried,
Within the church's shelter arched and aisled –
Peacefully wondering—to the alter carried.

White-robed and sweet, in semblance of a flower,
What as the daisies that adorned the chancel;
Borne like a gift-the young wife's natural dower –
Offered to God as her most precious Hansel."

— "Christening," by George Parsons Lathrop, *Congregationalist,* June 7, 1900

A scalloped swag motif on pre-embroidered yardage becomes the design focus on this gown's yoke when lace edging repeats the elegant line. Not only should the sense of creative design be applauded, but the idea of shaping lace edging rather than insertion lends a softer, almost Tiffany-like effect to the overall look of the piece.

The style is a low-yoke sized to leave room beneath the embroidery design for the application of the Swiss beading that defines the high waist while centering the embroidered swags horizontally. The lace edging not only echoes the line, but its positioning cups the bottom of the sprays embroidered above the swags. The Swiss beading is an entredeux-edged design with a fernlike embroidery that makes a pretty coordinate to the pre-embroidered yardage. A narrower entredeux-edged beading topped with a slightly gathered French lace edging finishes the neckline. Both beadings are run with soft pink ribbon in widths that accommodate the openings and tie in back to close the dress at the neck and the waist.

The puffed sleeves are embellished with a loop of shaped lace edging around an embroidered motif; they are finished similarly to the neckline but have a slightly wider lace edging.

The back yokes are cut from the Swiss embroidered yardage set sideways so that the swags are mirror imaged beside the placket. Inside is a little label with the name

"Milsom" stitched in red.

A sad bit of history is attached to this and a number of pristine, Milsom-family pieces that are now a permanent part of the museum's clothing collection. The donor was going through his late parents' belongings and came across a very large packing crate: nobody knew what was in it, if anything. When opened it turned out to contain a baby's cradle and complete set of clothes. It was then that the donor recalled that his parents' first child, born while they

were stationed in India (his father, Harry Milsom, had been in the army) was a girl, Patricia, who had been born in 1916 with a disabling medical condition and had died at five days old. His parents had packed up the baby's cradle and all her baby clothes and shipped them back to the family home in the United Kingdom, where they had remained undisturbed for all those years. Mr. and Mrs. Milsom went on to have two healthy sons, but acquired everything needed for them afresh.

The skirt is fashioned from the Swiss embroidered fabric and is 31-inches long. The fancy band at the bottom of the skirt is a row of 3/4-inch-wide Swiss insertion that has a double entredeux edge on both sides and a row of 1-1/2-inch-wide French bobbin lace edging applied flat. Both laces are of stylistic serpentine motifs that were apparently chosen for their similarity.

The handmade dress is English lawn. The total back length is 37-1/2-inches.

Misc.48 (7) 1983
Gift of Professor S.F.C. Milsom

Creative Inspiration

Machine embroider the lower part of a yoke with an antique-look, scalloped design, and echo the line with shaped edging lace with a smaller scalloped finish. The medley of scalloped work creates truly elegant detailing, and the same could be done on a sleeve or skirt hem.

White Violets Gown

Irish, 1910

"Are the violets already here!
Show me! I tremble so much to hear it, that even now
on the threshold of spring, I fear I shall die.
Show me the violets that are out."
— Excerpt, "Craving for Spring," by D.H. Lawrence

Naturalistic violets and their delicate foliage are sprinkled by means of hand embroidery on the bib inset, cuffs and waistband of this pretty white lawn baby gown. It was first worn by Diana Hamilton, who was born in 1910, and then by her sisters, Noreen, born 1913, and Cecilia, born three years later. Various meanings have been attached to flowers, particularly during Victorian times, and the white violet is often associated with youthful innocence, faithfulness and a chance for happiness. Perhaps the motif was chosen with these qualities in mind. Or it could have been a favorite flower. Then again, violets may have held no special meaning to the seamstress and were simply a product of an embroidery template, as designs were readily available in books and magazines of the day.

The to-the-waist dress with bib-shaped inset at the neck – the embroidered piece – is joined at the sides and bottom with tiny entredeux, traced with a bias band of speckle embroidery and a slightly gathered French-lace edging. The framework around the inset gives the impression that the gown has a separate midyoke because it conceals the fact that there is no midyoke seam. The top of the inset serves as the neckline, which is finished in baby entredeux, a band of bias trim and a slightly gathered French edging. The long puffed sleeves have a similar finish – a cuff trimmed at the top and bottom with the bias band and slightly gathered lace edging. The cuffs fasten with linen-covered buttons and stitched loops.

The fullness in the body of the gown is gathered between the bib inset and the embroidered waistband panel to create a section of shirring. Lace-hemmed sashes of self-fabric attached at each side of the waist panel tie in a back bow. The bodice back has lines of shirring at the neck, and the fullness of fabric between shoulders and waist is pulled into unpressed pleats. The gathered skirt is finished with horizontal tucking – three rows of two 1/8-inch-wide tucks placed 1/2-inch apart and a fourth row

of three tucks – and a fancy band that consists of a single row of French lace insertion, horizontal tucking – a grouping of three tucks, then two tucks – and finally a 2-3/4-inch-deep lace-edged flounce, which has been fluted by an ironing technique. The flounce is embellished with two sections of two 1/16-inch-wide horizontal tucks, and the join is topped with additional bias banding of speckle embroidery.

The gown fastens in back with neck and waist drawstrings, linen-covered buttons and stitched buttonholes. The gown is 28-inches long; the circumference of the skirt is 68-inches. The seams are French, and the gown was constructed entirely by hand.

"Jermy Gwyn," perhaps an owner's mark, is found inside the gown, but no information is given regarding the significance of the name. Often, pieces were marked to indicate which side of the family a gown came from or sometimes to note that it was to go back to someone else.

Misc.216-1983
Gift of Noreen Hamilton and her sisters, Diana and Cecilia Hamilton-Wedderburn

Creative Inspiration
Embroider several waistband panels with different seasonal motifs, and add self-fabric ties to the sides; interchangeable sashes add versatility to an heirloom-sewn dress.

Kimono Sleeve Netting Gown and Bonnet

British, 1937

"Children should not be rocked or patted off to sleep, but simply laid in their cots; and if for the first night or two they cry a little, this will not hurt them, but will rather be good mental discipline for the future; they will soon gain the habit of sleeping without external help."
— From Cradle to School, A Book for Mothers, by the Late Mrs. Ada A. Ballin,
©1902 Constable and Company, London

The understated beauty of this christening gown lies in the simple silhouette and the ivory lace fabric. Use of a kimono-sleeve style for a christening is rather unusual, although this piece is dated much later than most of the other gowns in this book. It is understandable why Mrs. Gladys Murdoch, the seamstress, chose not to cut into the lace pattern anymore than necessary. It is exquisite netting lace yardage with a dramatic design that is increasingly dense with floral detailing as it pours toward the scalloped hem. Mrs.

Murdoch made the christening gown and bonnet for her daughter Elizabeth Marion born in 1937.

The bodice is cut from the lower part of the lace yardage so that the scalloping falls at the slightly raised waist, front and back. The kimono sleeves and round neckline are trimmed in ivory lace edging. The sleeves are also trimmed with a bow and a knotted loop of ivory satin baby ribbon. The skirt is a single width of lace seamed down the center back, 55-inches in circumference. It is gathered to the bodice and is trimmed to the left of the waist center with a multilooped bow of ivory satin baby ribbon with streamers. The gown fastens in back with three pearl buttons and stitched loops. The dress is 29-inches long.

The simple Japanese silk undergown has a drawstring finish at the neck and kimono-sleeve edges. The skirt is lightly gathered to the high-waist bodice and is finished in a plain hem.

The bonnet is cut from the lace yardage and is gathered onto a round crown piece in back. It is lined in ivory Japanese silk. The front edge is trimmed with two rows of lace frill and is edged with two double rows of pleated white net. The bonnet fastens with tying strings of ivory satin ribbon falling from beneath rosettes of ivory satin baby ribbon.

Misc.711 (1,2,3)-1992
Gift of Mrs. Gladys Murdoch

Butterflies Gown
English, 1923

"Oh! pleasant, pleasant were the days,

The time, when, in our childish plays,

My sister Emmeline and I

Together chased the butterfly!

A very hunter did I rush

Upon the prey:—with leaps and springs

I followed on from brake to bush;

But she, God love her, feared to brush

The dust from off its wings."

—Excerpt from "To a Butterfly," by William Wordsworth

A high-waist gown of white lawn, this piece exemplifies the ingenuity and frugal nature of the home seamstress. The pre-embroidered lawn quite likely came from a factory that mass-produced embellished yardage for women's blouses. Elizabeth Charlotte Weller, born 1896, worked as a sample hand making women's sample blouses of the new styles, an indication that she was a skilled professional seamstress used to producing delicate and decorative work. Her job appears to have given her access to some unusual fabrics (employers in the clothing industry made presents to their staff of fabric for wedding or baby apparel). From where the firm sourced their fabrics is unknown: the fabric and blouses would not have been made in the same factory. The museum owns the layette of 17 day garments that the seamstress made for her baby daughter Renee Weller (the donor).

The bodice is a combination of vertical tucked sections alternating with rows of French lace beading. The same beading joins the bodice to the gathered skirt and forms the sleeve cuff, but in these areas it is run with a tiny pink satin ribbon. The neckline is finished with a bias binding and topped with a row of slightly gathered French lace edging, the same edging that finishes the sleeves. The design of the back bodice is the same as that of the front and closes with buttons and buttonholes. A butterfly motif is a perfectly lovely choice for a baby gown, particularly if this one were worn for a christening, as butterflies symbolize rebirth and new beginnings. The primary design is naturalistic embroidery of butterflies and roses with a Chinoiserie feel. The hem resembles the geometric fretwork motifs customarily worked on Chinoiserie furniture.

The gown is 31-1/2-inches long.

Misc.75(5)-1976
Gift of Miss Renee Weller

Feathers and Flowers Gown
English, 1820-30

"The first thing to be taken care of, is, that children be not too warmly clad or covered, winter or summer. There are those in England who wear the same clothes winter and summer and that without any inconvenience, or more sense of cold then others find."
—"Treatment of Children," *Weekly Visitor and Ladies' Museum*, May 1822

Most of the Ayrshire work on this elegant gown, or robe as it would have been called in the earlier part of the 1800s, would fall into the category of a sprig design for obvious reasons. The excessive sleeves emphasized by the bodice robings are also typical of the period, a time when large sleeves and bell-shaped skirts were the norm in adult dress. Although curator Noreen Marshall does not subscribe to the notion that children were dressed like miniature adults, she nevertheless concurs that children's and adults' clothing always have likenesses. One exception on this particular piece is the absence of robings down the skirt. Instead, the embroidery simply forms a triangular line to convey the tradition of a center panel.

The gown has its original skirt and bodice, but there is an interesting alteration. Many of these pieces came from wealthier families, and there was a certain amount of veneration among them, as well as a certain amount of thrift ingrained in them. They had the money and kept it; it would have gone to the estate or the children's education or training rather than to replace things they could make do with or mend. This gown exemplifies frugality and at the same time shows the drawback of Ayrshire embroidery. The embroidery technique, which involves cutting holes in the fabric, puts quite a bit of strain on the surface. In other words, Ayrshire is decorative weakness. This bodice was substantially repaired with netting to reinforce the Ayrshire, and a section of embroidered edging was added around the waistline. The dress may have been torn in this area, making it necessary to apply patching directly on top of the bodice robing.

The narrow band that tops the waist seam would have been added later as well, because it is worked on top of the waistline patch. The casing is topped with a tiny line of very closely worked French knots to echo a similar treatment around the neckline.

The unusual sleeves are seamed down the center to form a double puff that resembles a butterfly and cuffed with a narrow band of embroidered fabric. The waistline closes with two covered buttons and button loops. The plain hem on the skirt is 3-1/2-inches deep. The dress is 39-1/2-inches long with a circumference of 36-inches.

Circ.410-1924
Gift of Mrs. Frances Maddams

Crossed Columns Gown
English, 1890-93

"In England baby clothes are made for the first month of the baby's life, for the second month, the third, and so on; and as the infant grows out of one set, it is put away, and for the next set used. One outfit thus suffices for several successive claimants."
—"Baby Clothes," *Christian Advocate*, May 28, 1991

The manner in which this piece is constructed, with the extensive Swiss embellishment concentrated at the center front, makes it look as if it were a separate gown and pinafore. The wide van Dyke edging that outlines the hourglass shape of the front panel reinforces the impression. The gown is a typical silhouette used in the latter part of the 19th century, when the princess line emphasized a small waistline. The placement of vertical insertions, both a 2-1/4-inch-wide Swiss embroidery and a narrower 3/4-inch-wide French lace, draw the silhouette inward in the upper part of the gown, while the horizontal bands of Swiss embroideries and van Dyke flounces give the skirt a sense of fullness as the work continues towards the hem. It is actually 26-inches at its widest point, including the edging. While the panel is made up mostly of joined bands of laces, the fabric sections underneath the double flounces are unadorned cotton panels.

The scooped neckline is finished in narrow French lace stitched on underneath a casing that closes in the back with a pull cord; similar casings are worked at the sides of the waist, but run only to the edges of the hourglass panel and not through it so that when the cords are tied, the gown does not gather across the front. All the casings are topped with a line of tiny French knots. The long sleeves have a pretty cuff created from a length of Swiss insertion with entredeux edges. The seamstress incorporated the seam tape of the entredeux into the cuff design by topping it with a hand featherstitch and seaming it to the gathered sleeve on one side and to slightly gathered French edging on the other. She worked a little placket at the wrist that closes with a tiny pearl button and loop.

The back of the skirt is unadorned except for a single set of narrow tucks at the bottom and a flat fancy band of the wide Swiss insertion and edging. The back length of the gown is 37-1/2-inches long. Inside the back bodice is a little label with the initials "HD" stitched in red. This may have been a family mark to indicate to whom the gown should be returned.

The donor said that she believed the gown was made for her grandmother (née Cecily Evelyn Gordon Besley, born about 1893). Miss Daniell's gift included a carrying cape, a bonnet and another dress, as well as this one, and she wrote that the two dresses were the only surviving Besley family baby clothes "because they were sent to South Africa for me when I was born in 1921 (there is a small Cash's nametape on one with the initials 'HD'– my mother was Henriette Daniell). I never wore them because [it was] too hot, but that is how they were kept separately from the rest." Noreen Marshall's recollection is that the donor said that "the rest" were destroyed in a house fire at the family home.

Misc.359-1979
Gift of Miss D. Daniell

Ribbon Slot Gown
British, 1921

"The white robe which a baby traditionally wears for his baptism represents the new life, free from sin, into which he has been spiritually reborn."
—*Yesterday's Children: The Antiques and History of Childcare*, by Sally Kevill-Davies,
© March 1992, Antique Collectors' Club

The English word for beading is ribbon slot, hence the name of this robe. The particular Swiss beading is quite wide and would accommodate a 1-inch ribbon, although in its current state, no ribbon is included in the design. The design on the skirt edging and insertion laces match. The insertion on the bodice and sleeves and the edging around the neckline and wrist are a very simple coordinate design, and all the laces have an airy net foundation. The remaining trims on the robe include a touch of entredeux at the wrist and an entredeux-edged Swiss trim that joins the skirt to the bodice.

The bodice is designed around a central mitered lace V. Above the lace is a fabric V filled with a delicate spray of hand embroidery that follows the shape. The neckline is finished in a compound scalloped edge in front and entredeux in back; slightly gathered lace edging is applied to both. Beneath the lace V are diagonally placed fabric sections of three tucks flanked by rows of French knots alternating with lace insertion. The lace-insertion motif is simply a row of dots on a netting foundation, so the rows of French knots mirror this design. A single lace insertion V also trims the sleeves, and here the French knots follow the lace shape above and below. The knots are worked so that the thread carries from one knot to the next on the back side, and this shadows through the diaphanous fabric. The embellishment on the back bodices runs vertically. At the center of each is the narrow Swiss trim between two rows of French-lace edging, two rows of French knots and two sections of three tucks. The simple placket closes at the neck and at the waist with a single flat pearl button and loop.

The skirt consists of three tiers. The first is 17-inches deep and is trimmed at the bottom with a row of French knots between two sections of three 1/16-inch tucks. The second tier is 8-5/8-inches deep and is trimmed completely around with spires of hand-embroidered floral designs that run the entire depth. The third tier is a 3-inch-deep fabric flounce with three 1/16-inch tucks at the bottom and is finished with a 3-inch-wide netting lace edging. A row of 1-inch-wide lace insertion and the ribbon slot separate each tier.

The robe is 39-1/2-inches long, and the circumference of the skirt above the gathered flounce is 70-inches.

Misc.469-1992
Gift of Miss Stella Randall
(original wearer)

"Mothers are always complaining, 'Baby won't keep his boots on;' of course he won't if he can help it – they are too uncomfortable."
— From Cradle to School, A Book for Mothers, by the late Mrs. Ada A. Ballin,
©1902 Constable and Company, London

"I must insist that it is even more important for children than for adults that their feet should be properly clad; yet whenever I have spoken to a bootmaker on the subject he has said, 'We very rarely make boots for children to order; ladies prefer to buy them ready made and save expense.' "
— From Cradle to School, A Book for Mothers, by the late Mrs. Ada A. Ballin,
©1902 Constable and Company, London

"If we watch the movements of infants' feet, we notice their great freedom; the little toes are stretched out and drawn back; they will grasp anything placed in contact with them, and the bones and muscles are all brought into play in seemingly aimless sprawling."
— From Cradle to School, A Book for Mothers, by the late Mrs. Ada A. Ballin,
©1902 Constable and Company, London

Very little can compare with the sweetness of a baby's tiny toes, but exquisite French-made footwear comes astonishingly close. The three sets of footwear with colored embroidery are made of ribbed silk with a brushed-cotton insole and finished with a buttery leather sole. The rounded toes are intricately embroidered with naturalistic floral motifs. The embroidery on the two ballet-style shoes (in the center) vines around the quarter. Each fastens at the ankle with button-through straps. The blue shoes are trimmed across the throat with a ruched band and frill of blue ribbon. The ecru shoes are less ornately finished at the throat with a single gathered frill. The bias silk finish around the edges is applied with tiny handpicked stitches. The pale peach boot has no floral embroidery on the shaft, but ivory featherstitch in silk floss follows the arched line just beneath the silk bias and ribbon-frilled edge. An ivory ribbon ties the boot at the top. A lovely triple bow fashioned from the ribbed silk and adorned with a wreath of cut steel beads is set atop the throat. All three styles are a combination of machine work and handwork.

The fourth pair, an English-made, ballet-style shoe, is ecru cotton trimmed with soft grey eyelets and padded satin-stitch embellishment. These are unlined and less structured than their French counterparts but are very similar in silhouette. They fasten with an ankle strap that is secured with a tiny button and loop concealed beneath a little strap extension.

Left to Right:
French, 1880s
T.356 (A,B) 1960
Gift of Miss G. Porter

French, 1880
Misc.144 (1,2) 1985
Gift of Miss Beryl Hinton

French, 1880-90
Misc.939 (1,2) 1988
Gift of Susan Newby Robson

English, 1916
Misc.48 (38A,B) 1983
Gift of Professor S. F. C. Milsom

Daisy Rows Gown

English, 1880-1900

"I have seen a lovely christening robe made from my pattern, trimmed with real Valenciennes lace and embroidered in washing silks in a pattern of daisies. The robe is to be cut thirty inches long, and twenty eight at the bottom, giving a circumference of forty-six inches, so as to allow plenty of room for kicking."
—From *Cradle to School, A Book for Mothers,* by the Late Mrs. Ada A. Ballin,
©1902 Constable and Company, London

Robings, or ruffles, positioned down the sides of a baby gown were originally inspired by mainstream fashion of the period. Although these distinguishing adornments have all but disappeared in adult dress, robings on christening attire evolved into a traditional style that is still used today. The robings on this gown are applied in a dual fashion. The main set runs down the sides of the center panel, which is a customary placement. The second set edges the inverted V inset on the lower part of the skirt. Robings that finish below the waistline are not unusual, but having both sets in the same gown is very much out of the ordinary.

Three laces are used throughout. A narrow French edging around the neckline casing and the sleeve band, a 1-1/2-inch-wide daisy insertion edged with a drawn-thread border, and a wide Swiss edging cut in varying widths, depending upon whether it is used for the flounces, the robings or the hem around the back of the skirt. The center front panel is pieced together in several sections. Starting at the neckline, three vertical strips of insertion are shaped into an hourglass silhouette; the fabric between the insertions is either topped with featherstitching (at the neckline) or folded into 1/4-inch-wide tucks spaced 3/8-inch apart (from the waist to midway down the skirt).

The inverted V panel on the skirt begins approximately a third of the way down the gown. The top half of the panel is shaped from mitered Swiss insertion traced with the Swiss edging; the V meets the side robings about halfway down the panel where the insert levels off and falls straight to the hem. The banding inside this lower panel alternates Swiss edging and flat fabric sections topped with Swiss edging flounces of graduating widths; the first flounce is barely 2-inches across the top, and the final flounce is 21-1/2-inches wide. All the Swiss is joined in the same fashion, with the selvedge turned under, placed on top of the adjoining piece and straight-stitched close to the edge.

The scooped-neck bodice and waist both incorporate a casing and pull cord, which secure the gown in back. The skirt beyond the center panel is finished around the bottom with three 1/4-inch-wide tucks, a 1-inch hem and a continuation of the Swiss edging that finishes the front panel. The entire gown is stitched by machine, and the inside seams are unfinished. The gown is 35-inches long.

Misc.16-1983
Gift of Mrs. F. E. Baverstock

Converted Betrothal Vest
English, 1820-30

"Children are but little people, yet they form a very important part of society, expend much of our capital, have considerable influence on the corn-laws, employ a great portion of our population in their service, and occupy half the literature of our day in labours or their instruction and amusement."

— "Childhood," *The Museum of Foreign Literature, Science, and Art,* March 1830

Made of ecru satin, this vest was presumably a gift to a young man for his engagement. The flowers are symbolic of early affection. Roses mean love and rosebuds, therefore, love in its early stages or a confession of love; pansies stand for thoughts and forget-me-nots, for true love or remembrance. In this combination, they suggest that the vest, originally embroidered as adult size, was probably intended as a betrothal gift. In its current state, the vest is smaller,

perhaps cut down to fit a child who wore it later. It came to the museum grouped with a rich blue suit and cream shirt. This suit would have been an "occasion" garment worn for events or family photographs.

The shawl collar design with welted pockets fastens in front with six satin-covered buttons and stitched buttonholes. The front and back are lined with ivory twill. Bound brass eyelets in the back are laced with tapes that can be drawn up to make the garment fit more snugly. The colored silk sprays of rosebuds, forget-me-nots and pansies are worked in crewel stitch.

Misc.227 (4) –1979
Gift of Mr. John Tayleur

Creative Inspiration
Machine embroider a nearly identical style vest for a woman to pair with a sheer, full-sleeve blouse and a skirt or dress pants.

Royal Baby Gift Box

English, 1923

"I am desired by the Princess Mary to acknowledge the receipt of your letter of the 19th of February and to ask you to convey to W. Day thanks for the charming silk box containing the baby shoes and socks with which Her Royal Highness is much pleased and she greatly appreciates W. Day's kind thought in sending them to her. Believe me Yours truly, Dorothy Yorke, Lady in Waiting."
— Letter accompanying the box, dated March 19th 1923

There is a reason this exquisite gift box filled with baby essentials was returned to Mrs. Day. It was intended to be worn by the firstborn child of Her Royal Highness Princess Mary of York, great-granddaughter of Queen Victoria. However the baby, born February 7, 1923, was a boy, George, as was the second child, Gerald. The original letter of gratitude was penned by one of the Princess's ladies in waiting and has remained with the box and its contents.

The box is covered in a shell pink ribbed silk and trimmed with a large pink satin bow. The interior is lined with flat sugar pink silk. Two 3/8-inch satin carrying ribbons finished with 1/8-inch ribbon bows at each end extend across the inside lid. The ribbons are tacked to the lid in two places to create holders for three pairs of socks (two pink and one white machine-knitted silk with cotton heels and toes) and a pair of pink satin ballet slippers in a pochette (a small pink satin bag with white satin lining). A second length of the 1/4-inch ribbon tacked to one side keeps the lid from opening too wide. The box is divided into three compartments, one each for the pairs of shoes - a gold kid leather slipper, a quilted lace-covered boot and

pink satin moccasin.

The tiny moccasins are made of pink satin. The ribbon tie is tacked to the interior counter and laced through openings next to the tongue. When tied, the ribbon fastens around baby's ankle and ideally keeps the moccasin from falling off. The gold slippers with a 3/4-lining of white kid leather, fasten around the ankle, but there is no apparent closure. The soles are white suede. The boots are cream crocheted lace over pink silk and finished with bias silk binding and matching lace edging that the ends in a lace

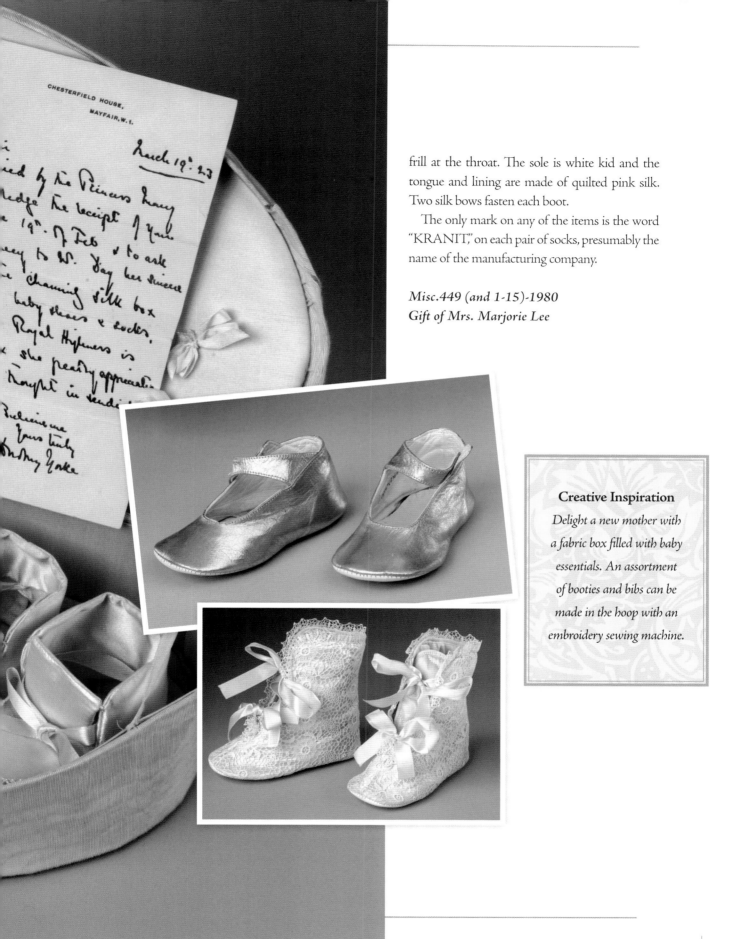

frill at the throat. The sole is white kid and the tongue and lining are made of quilted pink silk. Two silk bows fasten each boot.

The only mark on any of the items is the word "KRANIT," on each pair of socks, presumably the name of the manufacturing company.

Misc.449 (and 1-15)-1980
Gift of Mrs. Marjorie Lee

Creative Inspiration
Delight a new mother with a fabric box filled with baby essentials. An assortment of booties and bibs can be made in the hoop with an embroidery sewing machine.

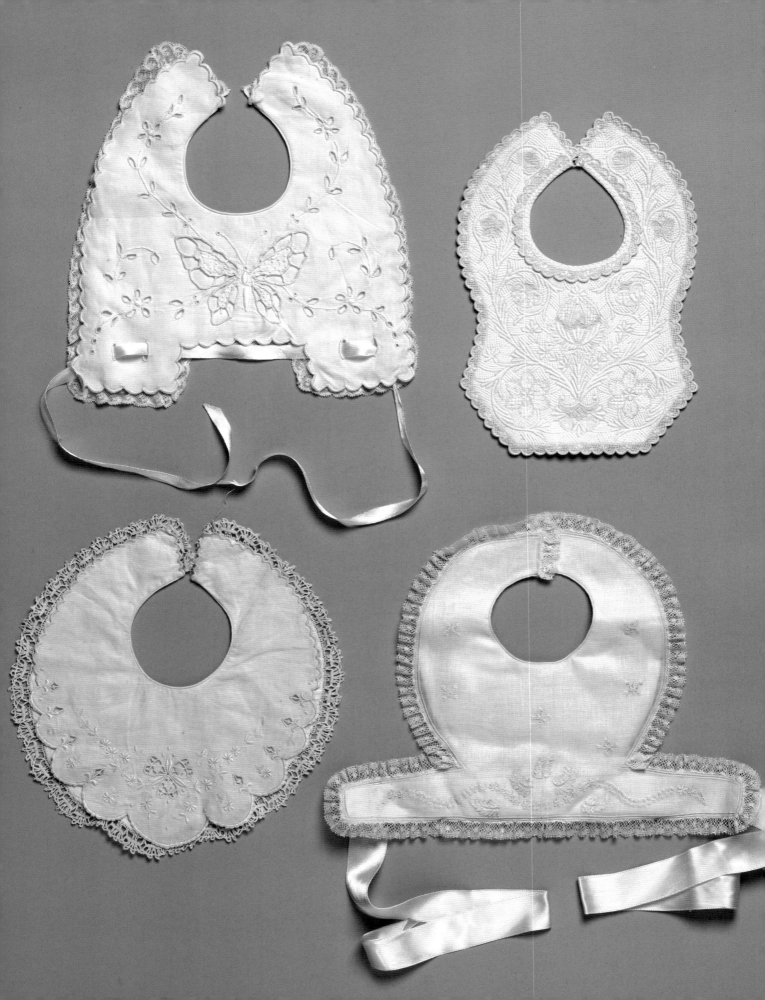

Bibs

"The Countess of Romney presides over a stall devoted to the sale of little children's clothes — little frocks, drawers, knitted petticoats, babies' socks, caps, bibs, and all the paraphernalia of infanthood. At another stall is seen Miss Eardley Wilmot, one of the reigning beauties of London society."
— "A Fashionable Fair in Piccadilly," by Olive Logan, *Harper's Bazaar*, January 18, 1879

Four bibs in distinctly different shapes and adornment techniques exemplify the lengths to which loved ones would go with a needle and thread to assure baby was aptly outfitted. The time and effort poured into a bib was nearly as extensive as that given to baby's clothing.

The linen cutwork bib (upper left) consists of two layers, a plain underlayer trimmed with a slightly gathered French lace edging and a top layer embellished with a beautiful butterfly cutwork design and scalloped edge. The tab extensions at the bottom each have two buttonholes through which a satin ribbon is woven to secure the bib around baby's chest.

The padded matelassé bib (upper right) is a combination of the tiniest quilting stitches in an allover pattern, needlework appliqués and openwork backed with sections of drawn thread. A scalloped trim of drawn thread work finishes the edges of the bib and is applied around the neckline, which is finished with a bias band topped with featherstitch. The bib fastens with a flat pearl button and loop. Records indicate that it was made by Miss van Loest, a superintendent at one of Dr. Barnardo's homes for children*. Apparently, she was inspired by a piece of 18th-century embroidery.

The most delicate of the collection (lower right) is a pretty French bib made of white linen. The round-neck design takes the continental form (popular from the 1920s), a simple circular bib with a bottom band. The cotton lining is left open at the sides of the band, and a pink ribbon is threaded through the layers to tie the bib around baby's chest. The lightweight linen allows the pretty pink satin ribbon to shadow through and further emphasizes the decorative work — chain-stitched fern foliage around a serpentine spray of daises and French knots. Additional daisies are scattered on the circular part of the bib. Two rows of tiny chain stitch outline the bib shape, with the outer row used to secure a perfectly pleated French lace edging finish. The neck is piped with a self fabric. A single button and loop closes the bib at the neck and is concealed beneath the lace edging. A dribble-catcher on the underside of the bib is made of white linen padded with

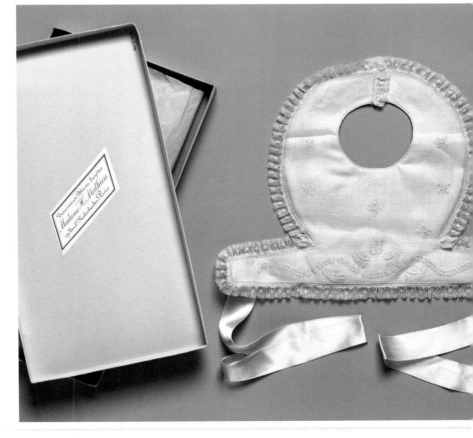

wadding. This particular bib was commercially made for Madame H. Mathieu's shop at 19 Boulevard Malesherbes, Paris; the shop owner's tag is tacked to the back side. It has survived with its original box, a rectangular buff cardboard covered in pale blue paper with a detachable white lid covered in pale pink paper.

The Cluny lace bib (lower left) is made up of two ivory linen layers, a plain underlayer trimmed in Cluny lace and a top layer finished in a scalloped edge. The scallops are stitched so that the center front scallop is the widest, and succeeding scallops become gradually smaller to about the midway point, where the scallops reduce to barely 1/4-inch wide and continue completely around to the back neck opening. Cutwork with a Cluny trefoil insert, satin stitch embroidery and a single eyelet are worked at the center front of the bib. Whitework posies and leaves vine outward from this motif. Centered in the side scallops are whitework posies, and each of these scallops is crowned with a tiny whitework motif and a small cutwork diamond. The neckline is piped, and there is no apparent closure. The bib was made by the donor's French nanny, Henriette Cousseau.

* *Dr. Thomas Barnardo, who was born in Ireland and sought his higher education in London, founded the East End Mission for impoverished children in 1867; it and similar facilities came to be known as Dr. Barnardo's Homes.*

Creative Inspiration

Make up a collection of baby bibs, each featuring a different shape and different embellishment techniques. They're the perfect size samplers to polish handwork skills or to test machine embroidery designs.

Clockwise

English, 1880-1900
Circ.14 -1936
Gift of Miss M. J. van Loest via Miss B. K. Baillie

French, 1963
B.936:1-1993
Gift of Mrs. Marie-Claude Willis

French, 1918
Misc.767-1986
Gift of Mrs. M. Mason

French, 1920
B.157: 1-1999
Gift of Mr. & Mrs. Herbert Ruben

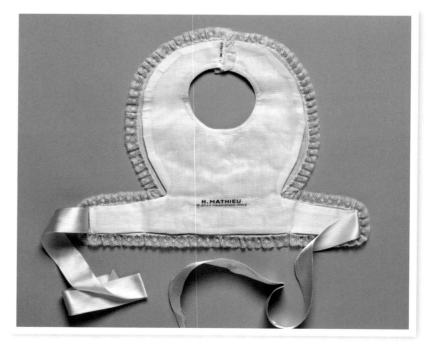

Ruched Netting Matinee Jacket and Pink Rosettes Bonnet

Hungarian, 1920-29

"Not much hope had she, however, that her mother would let her have a new organdy, but she'd look at them anyway. And look at them she certainly did Flowered organdies in every shade of pink, blue lavender, green, and yellow the obliging clerk held up for the two girls — in the most fascinating folds... Really it must have been a full half hour before May finally decided on a rose pink one."

— "Parking Mrs. Blossom's Baby," by Dora Dexter, from *The Continent*, reprinted in *Herald of Gospel Liberty*, June 24, 1926

At the time the donor purchased this precious pink set in a "baby clothes shop" in Budapest, she was expecting her first child, and baby clothes were in very short supply. The year was 1943, and even then, these pieces were sold as antiques. Museum documentation records her comment that "she did not realize then how impractical they were, and they were not used for any of her children, Wanda, Beatrix, or (for obvious reasons) Thomas."

The jacket is ivory net over a lining of pale pink silk with a lace-edged hem. It has a turned-down Peter Pan collar and wrist-length sleeves with turned-back cuffs. The collar and hem are hand embroidered with floral sprays in matching silks. The garment fastens at the neck front with a button and stitched loop. Of special interest in the construction of this jacket is the net ruching or puffing applied around the jacket bottom, the cuffs and the collar. The strip around the jacket bottom is 7/8-inch wide and those on the collar and cuffs are 1/2-inch wide. The back length is 11-1/2-inches.

It is doubtful that the bonnet, probably among the prettiest pieces in the museum collection, was originally made as a part of the set. Even though both pieces share a color scheme, pink silk with ecru lace trim, the bonnet is crepe (lined with flat pink silk), and the bonnet laces, although French, do not match the edging used on the jacket. The mixing of laces is not a definitive clue of their provenance, but the embroidery seems to be; although the stitching styles are similar, the motif on the jacket is daisies

and vines worked in ecru cotton floss, and the designs on the bonnet are rose bouquets and swags worked in pink silk floss.

The bonnet is gathered to a self-piped circular crown, which is embroidered with a floral swag, a small bouquet and French knots. Piping also traces the bonnet completely around the edges as does a gathered 1-inch lace applied between the lining and bonnet. A band of tightly pleated silk, edged in 1/2-inch-wide lace, serves as an interior frill and is applied with a strip of self-bias tape. Softly shaped scallops of 1/2-inch-wide lace insertion are set in mirror image on the head piece. Sprays, swags and bouquets of tone-on-tone silk embroidery are worked in harmony with the lace shaping. Absolutely elegant ribbon flowers — two large and six small — in the exact shade of silk are tacked along the front of the bonnet and linked together by a twisted ribbon rope over wire that hangs loosely between each flower. A single tying string of silk ribbon is looped, tucked and tacked to the insides of the bonnet edge.

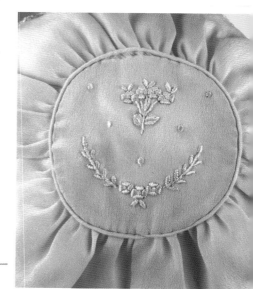

B.381-1993
B.382-1993
Gift of Frau Ilona Hirsch

Ecru Eyelet Romper
British, 1820-25

"Boys and girls should be dressed alike until the boys are breeched, and when they begin to walk a change may be made from the baby dress."
— From *Cradle to School, A Book for Mother*, by the Late Mrs. Ada A. Ballin,
©1902 Constable and Company, London

A small boy would have worn a romper of this nature as an everyday garment during the mid to late 1800s, and relatively few utilitarian pieces like this have survived, particularly ones in such fine condition. It is possible this one was worn by an only child and never handed down to younger sibling. Or, perhaps the child was the only boy in the family. The donor summarily described it as his "grandfather's first suit."

The romper is constructed of very durable cotton, probably nankeen fabric manufactured in Nankeen, China, which can also account for the garment's longevity. The piece was clearly designed for a boy as it was constructed with the necessary opening in the crotch. This romper also embraces the feminine influence of robings, which run around the back neckline and continue over the shoulder to the waistband. A detail that evolved from women's dress, robings, as well as lacework, were viewed as gender neutral in children's wear. The deep neckline is square and finished with a casing and drawcord that ties in back. The bodice center panel is embellished with narrow braid, embroidered leaves and eyelets that follow the V shape of the panel. The work is substantially heavier than what would have been applied to a girl's bodice of the same silhouette. The van Dyke robings are finished in a compound scallop, eyelets and embroidered greenery. Identical work finishes the trousers along the bottom.

The waistband is trimmed with three rows of narrow braid and two large, round, thread-covered buttons applied at the bottom of the robings. Bold buttons are another indication that this was a boy's garment. The cuffs on the short puffed sleeves are embellished with three rows of braid. There are two long plackets down the side seams and the trousers button onto the bodice in back in order to drop the garment down for necessary reasons. In back, the waistband becomes a separate belt with a hook-and-eye fastening, and it conceals the back flap.

T.22-1943
Gift of Mr. W. Duff Stewart

Creative Inspiration
Carefully choose the fabrics and trimmings for boy's heirloom apparel as an indication of gender rather than focus on the silhouette or style of the garment.

Ribbon-Trimmed Boys Suit

English, 1908

"It was the week before little Willie's birthday, and he was on his knees at his bedside
petitioning Divine Providence for presents in a very loud voice.
'Please send me,' he shouted, 'a bicycle, a tool chest, a ---'
'What are you praying to loud for?' his younger brother interrupted, 'God ain't deaf.'
'I know he ain't,' said little Willie, winking towards the next room, 'but grandma is.'"
— "A Boy of Method," from London Opinion, *reprinted in*
New York Evening Sun, *January 22, 1920*

As the 20th century approached the end of its first decade, the style of short trousers for little boys was firmly established. By that time, even women were stepping into pants due to earlier attempts by Amelia Jenks Bloomer to introduce harem-style pants as an alternative to full skirts. (It took a little time, but by the turn of the century, pants had become part of women's sporting attire.)

A dressmaker most likely designed and constructed this classic boy's button-on suit. Although made a century ago, the style is one that heirloom seamstresses, particularly those in Southern parts of the United States, would have no qualms about making for their own young sons to wear to church or other dressy events.

The focal point of the design is a French loomed ribbon worked as part of the covered placket down the front of the white linen shirt. It hides a series of snap closures. The turned-back cuffs, collar and knee breeches are all a shade of blue linen that is virtually identical to the ribbon. Five 7/8-inch-wide knife pleats are folded towards the placket on either side of the shirt front. The shirt back is folded into 10 pleats, and the shirt fronts and back are bridged with a narrow shoulder yoke. The long sleeves are gathered at the top of the armscye and tucked into the turned back, contrast cuffs.

Both hand and machine stitching were used in the garment construction. Inside the blouse is the number "17," and inside the pants, the number "33." These could be sizing marks or possibly style numbers determined by the dressmaker.

T.156-1959
T.156A-1959
Gift of Mrs. Willy Etla Friederburg Seeley

Creative Inspiration

Seek out a gender-neutral ribbon and reproduce the suit as is, adding less fullness to the sleeves. Velvet short trousers would be suitable for holiday dressing or, in white, or cream and white, this style would be ideal for a ring bearer.

Ecru Girl's Sailor Dress

English, 1905

"Sailor dresses are chiefly worn by girls under ten, those for children of five or six being often made in fanciful styles that are pretty on young children but less suitable for older girls."
— *"Modes for Children," Myra's Journal of Dress and Fashion*, October 1, 1887

In 1846, Queen Victoria ordered a sailor suit made for 4-year-old Prince Albert Edward to wear on the royal yacht. So endearing was the child in his scaled-down uniform that he was immortalized in a portrait by Franz Xaver Winterhalter. Thus began the allure of nautical-inspired clothing, a perennial favorite for over 150 years.

This is an unusually formal take on a girl's sailor suit, and it would have been worn for church and parties. It is actually a sleeveless dress with an overblouse. The top of the sailor suit was referred to as a "blouse" even for boys, and the word was part of naval terminology for some time. This particular blouse opens all the way down the front, although the effect is completely concealed. Three buttons and buttonholes down the front placket lie beneath the sashes of the long silk ribbon bow; a button and loop at the lowered neckline is hidden underneath the collar; and a hook and eye at the waistline falls underneath the blousing of fabric created by the elasticated casing that finishes the garment at the hem.

A traditional sailor style, the collar is cut square in back; it is trimmed, however, with a rich cream-colored braid. White, red or navy was more commonly used as sailor-style trimmings. Three rows of the cream braid trim the deep cuffs and the top of the patch pocket.

The sleeveless dress is constructed with a rectangle of cream fabric or dickey topstitched directly to the beige drop-waist bodice in front only. The stand-up collar is also beige cotton and because it was not cut on the bias, it buckles at the rim along the edge of the top row of cream braid. The sleeveless finish is a self bias binding. A 1-1/2-inch grow tuck is folded into the bodice 2-inches above the skirt. The dress closes down a back placket with three flat buttons and buttonholes and at the back neck with a tiny pearl button and thread loop.

The skirt is pleated into the waist seam to form a single wide panel in front and successive knife pleats all the way around the back. It has a 3-inch hem and is trimmed with five rows of braid.

T.158-1969 *(top)*
T158A-1969 *(dress)*
Gift of Mrs E. J. Browning

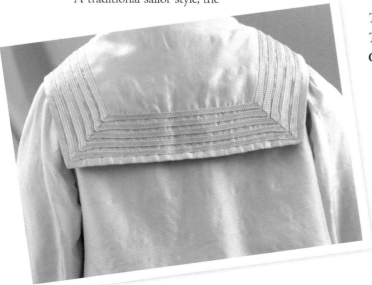

Creative Inspiration

Reproduce this two-piece sailor ensemble in identical fashion. The sleeveless dress underneath could be worn separately and, if desired, embellished with embroidery on the dickey/front panel for a completely different look.

Boy's Dress
English, 1905

"Very little boys under three wear blouse costumes with pleated skirts, blouses pleated throughout in the style of a Norfolk jacket, but reaching to the knees, or else pleated skirts with jackets over a full silk blouse plastron."
— *"Modes for Children," Myra's Journal,* July 1, 1888

Yes, this is a boy's garment, custom made for little Andrew Crookson, who was born in Scotland in about 1895. Records maintain the cream batiste dress and pale blue silk slip-dress were handmade in France and that Andrew wore the outfit as a child.

The round batiste yoke is trimmed with three strips of French-lace insertion that follow the circumference around to the back placket. A tiny featherstitch secures the lace to the fabric, which is trimmed from behind and allows the pale blue slip to shadow through. A fourth piece of lace encircles the round neck and is topped with a coordinate edging applied flat. The dropped-waist bodice is fashioned with 42 vertical tucks each just over 1/8-inch wide – 21 folded to the left and 21 folded to the right of center. The 3/4-length sleeves are finished in a lace cuff that comprises two strips of insertion lace and a strip of lace edging.

The gathered skirt joins the bodice with entredeux, and it is finished approximately halfway down with a wide fancy band – a strip of 1-inch-wide insertion lace, a fabric band of five 1/8-inch-wide horizontal tucks and a 3-1/2-inch-wide piece of French-lace edging applied flat. Pale blue silk ribbons are tied into double bows with long streamers and are tacked to the dropped waistline, one at each hip. The back of the dress is identical to the front except for a button placket and the absence of the silk ribbon bows.

The silk slip, or underdress, is cut from the same pattern as the embellished overdress, but it has limited design interest or trim. The plain, dropped-waist bodice is finished around the neckline with a self bias binding and a slightly gathered lace edging. The sleeves are set in with entredeux, and the lace cuff although similar to that on the dress has a single strip of insertion instead of two. The gathered skirt is seamed to the bodice without entredeux, and the skirt hem is finished with three horizontal tucks and a row of 1-7/8-inch-wide lace edging. Like the dress, it closes down the back placket with four buttons and buttonholes.

The center back length of the dress is 25-inches, and the skirt circumference is 90-inches.

Misc.780: 1-1986 (dress)
Misc.780: 2-1986 (blue slip)
Gift of Mrs. M. Mead

The Latter-Axton Dress

English, 1890

"Quite tiny children between one and three are best attired in cream or coloured flannel, Liberty silk, or woolen art fabrics. The little bodices are exceedingly pretty with a full yoke, smocked across the chest and back, and again at the waist."
— "Modes for Children," *Myra's Journal*, October 1, 1888

Coming from the Latter Axton estate, this terra-cotta costume would have been made for a little girl to wear to a special occasion or possibly for a portrait. With certainty, the parents who would purchase such an outfit would have supported the aesthetic movement of the late 19th century, a return to handwork, natural fabrics and naturalistic motifs. This entire piece was hand-constructed and all the interior seams have a whipped-thread finish.

The garment is actually a cutaway coat worn over a smocked sleeveless underdress. The back of the dress is pieced together with a firm cotton, a much more prudent use of fabric for a part of the dress that is concealed beneath the coat. The two areas of smocking, one across the chest and the other at the waist, create a wide section of gaging in between. The smocking is worked only wide enough to fill in the coat opening. The unadorned skirt is gathered by the waist smocking in front and falls into three soft pleats down the center. A stand-up collar finishes the neckline, and the armcyes are finished with a turned and hemmed edge. The cotton back is pieced into a princess line and has a center placket that fastens with four buttons and buttonholes. The gathered cotton skirt is finished in back with a wide band of the terra-cotta silk, as the hem would be visible underneath the coat.

The cutaway coat has a stand-up collar that fastens in front with hooks and eyes. The collar, turned-back lapels and sleeve cuffs are adorned with naturalistic daisies and greenery. Two large pearl buttons applied purely for decorative purposes trim the coat on each side of the waist. The back of the coat is seamed into a princess line, and the back skirt is folded into a pleated bustle that is topped with an excessively large terra-cotta silk bow. Additional daisy embroidery vines down the sides of the coat and across the bottom, ending at the first pleat of

the bustle. Interestingly enough, part of the embroidery transfer can be seen near the coat hem, where the seamstress never finished her stitching. The back length of this costume is 23-inches.

The piece was given to the museum by Mrs. J. A. Latter-Axton, who designed for Marshall and Snelgrove, a department store on Oxford Street in London that operated from the early 1850s to the mid-1970s; it is believed to be a sample garment. Mrs. Later-Axton gave the museum several items, including a number of dressed dolls and two children's garments, which demonstrate her taste for rich effects and her skill at achieving them.

T.139-1930 Dress
Gift of Mrs. J. A. Latter-Axton

Creative Inspiration
Embroider naturalistic daisy sprays down a little girl's pleated-front dress for a springtime look that's both tailored and feminine.

Bluebonnet Dress

English, 1885

"Little tots from two to five attired in velvet or velveteen will be in the height of juvenile fashion."
—"Modes for Children," *Myra's Journal*, November 1, 1888

"The mixing of different materials added to the fussiness of girls' fashions in the 1880s."
—*History of Children's Costume*, by Elizabeth Ewing ©1977 London: Batsford

Perhaps one of the more unusual pieces in the collection, this printed cotton and blue velvet dress is unlikely the work of a novice. Whoever designed the piece was probably involved in the fashion industry or had retail connections because she clearly had access to different trims, bits and pieces. She likely did not have a lot of wealth and so may have used her ingenuity and learned to put things together creatively out of necessity.

The neckline, which is shirred, and the long undersleeve, which is gathered at the wrist, are both cream muslin.

The remainder of the dress is cut from screen-printed cotton, an all-over print of a little girl (head and shoulders) wearing a blue bonnet. Machine-made lace layered over strips of blue velvet is applied in lederhosen fashion over the dropped-waist bodice. The rectangle of printed fabric between the velvet bands is gathered at the top and shirred at the bottom. A frill of the printed fabric trims the squared neckline formed by the velvet bands. The short sleeves are poufed with pick-ups into a layered lace and velvet cuff. Two velvet bows are tacked to one sleeve, but only a half bow is on the other. Clearly the remaining bow parts became detached over time, probably because they were simply tacked and not solidly stitched in place.

The skirt is two layers of fabric manipulation; a puffed skirt of pick-ups over a pleated skirt, folded such that a single blue-bonnet girl is centered at the bottom of every pleat. A partial petticoat of organdy and lace gives the skirt additional fullness.

The back of the dress is identical to the front except for the center placket, which closes with flat pearl buttons and buttonholes. The dress is 21-inches long.

T.115-1958
Gift of Mrs. W. H. Nicholson

Prince Albert Edward's Dress

English, 1843

"Three years have gone by,

Since a baby was I,

Like you, in the arms of my mother:

My eyes were as blue

And my skin as fair, too;

There were many who loved their new brother.

But years and the sun

Their work has begun,

To make me more wise and less fair –

I shall love you, I know,

When older you grow,

And will lead you to school with great care."

—Excerpt from "Lines to a Very Young Personage," by M.M. E., *The Juvenile Miscellany,* May 1830

Prince Albert Edward's dress is one of only a few garments of royal heritage at the V&A Museum of Childhood. The image of His Royal Highness the Prince of Wales was captured in this exact silk frock and its accompanying sash in an 1843 portrait painted by Franz Xaver Winterhalter at Windsor Castle. Queen Victoria commissioned the portrait, which is part of the UK Royal Collection and generally can be viewed online at the Royal Collection website (http://www.royalcollection.org.uk).

What no longer remains with the outfit are the deep lace tucker worn at the neck and what appears to be some kind of clasp holding the sash together. But these would have been used with other items.

The dress is a very angular garment made of off-white ribbed silk with a wide, piped neckline that fastens with a hook and thread loop in back. On the bodice, plain robings angle from the waist, continue over the shoulder and angle into the center back waist, where the apex is topped with a thread-covered button nestled in a pillow of looped thread. Between the robings in front, two angular strips of piped fabric that resemble pleats flank a single, centered box pleat. The box pleat is interrupted by the piped waist seam but then continues down the skirt to the hem. It is topped with 11 more of the ornate buttons.

The skirt is folded into a large inverted pleat beside the center box pleat. Three piped self bands extend from the waist seam down the skirt, are mitered at graduating points and continue in a horizontal line completely around the skirt. They appear at first to be folded pleats, but they are actually separate folded strips of fabric applied with piping. Additional thread-covered buttons top each band at the miter point.

The short sleeves are topped with three piped bands and two thread-covered buttons. The entire garment is lined in plain silk. The piece came to the museum paired with the pleated silk sash trimmed with knotted fringe, which the prince wore with the dress.

T.20-1933
T.21-1933
Donated by the executors of Mrs. Watkins Roberts

EMBROIDERIES

The embroidery designs shown are a sampling of the patterns featured on the antique garments in the V&A Museum of Childhood collection. These may be enlarged for hand embroidery or two multi-format CDs containing over 90 designs are available for machine embroidery from Martha Pullen Company.

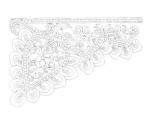

White Christmas Coat
and Capelet

White Christmas Coat
and Capelet

White Christmas Coat
and Capelet

White Christmas Coat
and Capelet

Candy Cane Dress

Candy Cane Dress

Candy Cane Dress

Candy Cane Dress

Candy Cane Dress

Pink Rosettes Bonnet

Pink Rosettes Bonnet

Flounced Tiers Gown